"Foremost expert in the international field of legal synaesthesia, Rostam Neuwirth reminds us in this engagingly complex critique of proposed EU regulation in AI systems, that in this age of paradox and oxymora, the mind, with its elaborately interactive sensory intersectionality involving cognition, knowledge, and reality, is a site precariously positioned for manipulation through systems of artificial intelligence that seek to control awareness and perception through subliminal techniques emboldened by irresponsible regulation. Law must protect our foundational freedom as humans to think, to feel, and engage with thoughts, feelings, and the reality that comes from this chaotic overlap."

Sarah Marusek, *University of Hawai'i Hilo (USA) and author of "Synesthetic Legalities: Sensory Dimensions of Law and Jurisprudence"*

"Rostam J. Neuwirth's book on the subliminal effects of AI is both original and timely. It is original because Neuwirth combines discourses from the fields of vulnerability theory, AI and neuroscience in a unique manner. The book is timely because the earlier one understands AI's subliminal effects, the higher is the chance that we can avoid that the concept of 'private thought' becomes an oxymoron. Neuwirth's latest book is thus essential reading for anyone committed to the protection of human dignity and human autonomy in the digital realm."

Valentin Jeutner, *Lund University (Sweden) and author of "Irresolvable Norm Conflicts in International Law: The Concept of a Legal Dilemma"*

"The global challenges of the XXI century spur humans to deal with Complex Systems. In my book, entitled 'Untangling Complex Systems: A Grand Challenge for Science', I show that Artificial Intelligence (AI) turns out to be a valuable tool to tackle Complexity. The development of AI brings humanity to the brink of a fourth technological revolution that will fundamentally alter the way humans live, work, and conceive themselves. There are intelligent machines that 'assist', others that 'augment' humans, and finally others that are 'autonomous'. These intelligent machines, which interact with humans, help face complex scenarios but raise ethical questions. The brilliant and farsighted Neuwirth's book presents the general context of the future regulation of AI. It specifically addresses the regulatory challenges related to the planned prohibition of 'the use of an AI system that deploys subliminal techniques beyond a person's consciousness'. Through a transdisciplinary examination of AI's legal, technological, linguistic and cognitive aspects, Neuwirth legitimately concludes that control of the mind should remain the personal domain of every human and the term 'private thought' should not become an oxymoron. Neuwirth's book is a 'must-read' for anyone who wants to know more about the regulation of subliminal AI systems."

Pier Luigi Gentili, *Department of Chemistry, Biology and Biotechnology, University of Perugia (Italy)*

"A highly important and timely discussion of the concept of subliminal manipulation at a time when the EU prepares to be one of the first major regulators of artificial intelligence. It is crucial that more experts like Professor Neuwirth contribute to the topic of reducing the risks of AI manipulation."

Risto Uuk, *Policy Researcher, Future of Life Institute (FLI)*

The EU Artificial Intelligence Act

AI in combination with other innovative technologies promises to bring unprecedented opportunities to all aspects of life. These technologies, however, hold great dangers, especially for the manipulation of the human mind, which have given rise to serious ethical concerns. Apart from some sectoral regulatory efforts to address these concerns, no regulatory framework for AI has yet been adopted, though in 2021 the European Commission of the EU published a draft Act on Artificial Intelligence and UNESCO followed suit with a Recommendation on the Ethics of Artificial Intelligence.

The book contextualises the future regulation of AI, specifically addressing the regulatory challenges relating to the planned prohibition of the use of AI systems that deploy subliminal techniques. The convergence of AI with various related technologies, such as brain–computer interfaces, functional magnetic resonance imaging, robotics, and big data, already allows for "mind reading" or "dream hacking" through brain spyware, as well as other practices that intrude on cognition and the right to freedom of thought. Future innovations will enhance the possibilities for manipulating thoughts and behaviour, and they threaten to cause serious harm to individuals as well as to society as a whole.

The issue of subliminal perception and the ability to deceive and manipulate the mind below the threshold of awareness causes severe difficulties for law and democracy and raises important questions for the future of society. This book shows how cognitive, technological, and legal questions are intrinsically interwoven, and aims to stimulate an urgently needed transdisciplinary and transnational debate between students, academics, practitioners, policymakers, and citizens interested not only in the law but also in disciplines including computer science, neuroscience, sociology, political science, marketing, and psychology.

Rostam J. Neuwirth is Professor of Law and Head of the Department of Global Legal Studies at the Faculty of Law of the University of Macau. Previously, he taught at the West Bengal University of Juridical Sciences (NUJS) in Kolkata and the Hidayatullah National Law University (HNLU) in Raipur (India), and worked as a legal adviser in the Department of European Law of the International Law Bureau of the Austrian Federal Ministry for Foreign Affairs. He received his PhD degree from the European University Institute (EUI) in Florence (Italy), and also holds a Master's degree in Law (LL.M.) from the Faculty of Law of McGill University in Montreal (Canada). As an undergraduate he studied at the University of Graz (Austria) and the Université d'Auvergne (France). He is the author of *Law in the Time of Oxymora: A Synaesthesia of Language, Logic and Law* (Routledge 2018) and numerous other publications that focus on contemporary global legal problems by exploring the intrinsic linkages between law, on the one hand, and language, cognition, art, culture, society, and technology, on the other.

Routledge Research in the Law of Emerging Technologies

Biometrics, Surveillance and the Law
Societies of Restricted Access, Discipline and Control
Sara M. Smyth

Artificial Intelligence, Healthcare, and the Law
Regulating Automation in Personal Care
Eduard Fosch-Villaronga

Health Data Privacy under the GDPR
Big Data Challenges and Regulatory Responses
Edited by Maria Tzanou

Regulating Artificial Intelligence
Binary Ethics and the Law
Dominika Ewa Harasimiuk and Tomasz Braun

Cryptocurrencies and Regulatory Challenge
Allan C. Hutchinson

Regulating Artificial Intelligence in Industry
Edited by Damian M. Bielicki

The Law of Global Digitality
Edited by Matthias C. Kettemann, Alexander Peukert and Indra Spiecker gen. Döhmann

Internet of Things and the Law
Legal Strategies for Consumer-Centric Smart Technologies
Guido Noto La Diega

The EU Artificial Intelligence Act
Regulating Subliminal AI Systems
Rostam J. Neuwirth

The EU Artificial Intelligence Act

Regulating Subliminal AI Systems

Rostam J. Neuwirth

Routledge
Taylor & Francis Group
LONDON AND NEW YORK

First published 2023
by Routledge
4 Park Square, Milton Park, Abingdon, Oxon OX14 4RN

and by Routledge
605 Third Avenue, New York, NY 10158

Routledge is an imprint of the Taylor & Francis Group, an informa business

British Library Cataloguing in Publication Data
A catalogue record for this book is available from the British Library

Library of Congress Cataloging-in-Publication Data
A catalog record has been requested for this book

ISBN: 978-1-032-33375-5 (hbk)
ISBN: 978-1-032-33383-0 (pbk)
ISBN: 978-1-003-31943-6 (ebk)

DOI: 10.4324/9781003319436

Typeset in Times New Roman
by Taylor & Francis Books

For Pui Mang

Contents

Preface

It is two years since Covid-19 was declared a global pandemic, and the many responses taken to combat the spread of the virus are said to have accelerated the development and use of new technologies commonly described as "artificial intelligence" (AI). Like the pandemic, the use of these new technologies has drastically altered the way we organize our lives, both publicly and privately, and has probably created a "new normal". However, in law the deeper and long-term effects of drastic changes usually take time to become visible and understood.

However, in dealing with change, law has the great benefit of an early warning system provided by science, technology, and language, which taken together offer significant insights into subtle or possibly subliminal trends that will inevitably make their appearance one day. My belief in this benefit was reinforced during research for my book *Law in the Time of Oxymora: A Synaesthesia of Language, Logic and Law* (Routledge 2018), and was recently confirmed when I reread the following from the preface to this book, which was originally drafted on 10 October 2017:

> In this world, the complexity and the accelerated pace of change equally threaten – like a *new pandemic global disease* – to undermine law, especially the rule of law as an instrument providing legal certainty and predictability.

Back then, little did I know about the metaphorical use of the word pandemic and even less did I expect the imminent outbreak of another global pandemic in the true sense of the word. In hindsight, however, it reminds me that changes in language detected in metaphors and oxymora – like changes in technologies – do provide a reliable indicator of hidden trends that will eventually surface. It is almost as if subtle linguistic changes function like "subliminal messages", or "hidden persuaders" as they are also known. In this sense, it is no coincidence that the term "artificial intelligence" (and numerous other concepts related to these new technologies) has repeatedly been described as an oxymoron.

This apparent coincidence prompted my interest in the research underlying this book, which was inspired, in general, by the publication by the European Commission of its Artificial Intelligence Act (AIA) and, in particular, by its proposed prohibition of AI systems that "*deploy subliminal techniques beyond a person's consciousness*". This planned prohibition marks, in my view, the key question for the future regulation of AI, because it directly addresses the cognitive seeds that these new technologies will plant through the various sensory channels in our minds. To put it differently, control over these technologies will mean control over (large parts) of the human mind and, when combined with big data and other technologies, tools or applications, will also mean control over the future.

From various historical examples we already know that cognitive change usually precedes political, institutional and other concrete changes encoded in laws and regulations. Paradoxically, the law also has a role in cognitive change, by making public the "hidden" processes that guide our thinking and influence our actions. This is why the law itself must adapt to the new possibilities created by artificial intelligence, which have been compared to "digital crystal balls" that allow the future to be predicted and that even assume the role of the creator of the world. Since most of these new technologies not only determine our lives in the so-called "black box society" but also penetrate into the hidden depths of the "black box" of our mind, it is in the mind that the law must initiate the quest for its constructive responses.

This book aims to make a constructive contribution to the quest for a new cognitive framework for law and legal reasoning. This is an immensely difficult task, given the complexity of all the relevant matters. Therefore, this book would never have been possible without the input, assistance, inspiration, and critical comments received from so many friends and colleagues and all the authors of the writings cited throughout this book. Here, I wish to express explicitly my sincere gratitude to Regis De Silva, Pier Luigi Gentili, Sara Migliorini, Tambiama Madiega, Valentin Jeutner, Isselmou Abdarahmane, Risto Uuk, and Li Yi for their constructive remarks on earlier versions, which helped me to have a better understanding of the complex and transdisciplinary underlying issues. For other forms of assistance, I am grateful to Mónica Ariño, Iris Eisenberger, Danny Friedmann, Alison Harcourt, Alexander Hartl, Stefan Rauschenberger, Nathalie Smuha, and Riccardo Vecellio Segate.

In the Faculty of Law of the University of Macau I am particularly grateful to Dean Tong Io Cheng, Wei Dan, Augusto Teixeira Garcia, Tu Guangjian, Perumal Ramaswamy, Alexandr Svetlicinii, Zhai Xiaobo, Du Li, Vera Lúcia Raposo, Isabel Mousinho de Figueiredo, Célia Filipa Ferreira Matias, Wenhua Xu, Chen Zhijie, and Denis de Castro Halis for the many fruitful discussions in the past, present, and future. In the University of Macau, I want to highlight explicitly the crucial role played by the Institute of Advanced Studies in Humanities and Social Sciences (IAS) and its fellows in fostering a truly transdisciplinary dialogue in all the meetings chaired by Vice-Rector Billy K.L. So and diligently organized by Amy Vong. I also received important inspiration from the participation in the first IAS annual conference entitled "Reflections across Disciplines: The China Story and Dialogue between Arts and Sciences" and particularly the presentation by Yu Xingzhong on a "Dialogue between Intelligent Technology and Law". Equally, important advice was received from the Center for Cognitive and Brain Sciences (CCBS) thanks to the assistance of Professors Zhen Yuan and Haiyan Wu. Here, I would also like to acknowledge the financial support received from the University of Macau by virtue of a Multi-Year Research Grant ("Law as 'Science Fiction': Future Regulatory Challenges from AI and other New Technologies" (MYRG2019–00017-FLL)).

Beyond the University, special thanks must go to my fellow co-editors Colin Picker, Junji Nakagawa, Meredith Kolsky Lewis, and Peter-Tobias Stoll and to all the contributors, for the inspiration to engage with future studies, in both utopian and dystopian ways, that emerged from the co-edited volume *A Post-WTO International Legal Order: Utopian, Dystopian and Other Scenarios* (Springer 2020). Equally, many thanks must go to Jingbo Huang, Serge Stinckwich, and Mamello Thinyane from the United Nations University (UNU) Institute in Macau for involving me in many important events related to this book. For important inspiration for the "law and technology" debate as well as the area of legal semiotics underlying the idea of legal synaesthesia, I would particularly like to thank Keiran Tranter, general editor of the journal *Law, Technology and Humans*, as well as Anne Wagner and Sarah Marusek, editors of the *International Journal for the Semiotics of Law* and the book series *Law and Visual Jurisprudence*, for including me in these novel and stimulating projects. I am equally grateful to the anonymous reviewers for their useful feedback and to Siobhán Poole, Sanjo J. Puthumana and Dominic Corti for guiding me speedily through the publication process.

Finally, my gratitude also extends to all friends and family who keep supporting me in all areas of life from afar, including Iris Neuwirth and her entire family, Olga Neuwirth, Gösta Neuwirth, Harald Neuwirth, Holger Neuwirth, Martin Kleiner, Stefan Meyer, Peter Griss, Robert Schütze, and Daniel and Brigitte Hollegha. Similarly, my heartfelt thanks to Pui Mang Cheong and our children Elam J. and Lea J. for both their support and their immense inspiration for this present book.

Rostam J. Neuwirth, Macao, 20 March 2022

Introduction

The Old Law restrains the hand, but the New Law controls the mind.[1]

There is a popular saying that "if you don't control your mind, the mind will control you!". To this, it could be added that if you do not control your mind, it is likely that someone else will control your mind for you. In this case, the fundamental question is whether the law should intervene to guarantee the freedom of the mind from attempts to control and manipulate it. In fact, the law already protects the mind from various forms of interference, most generally in the form of the right to freedom of thought and conscience. In addition, there are more specific laws and provisions that protect the mind from potentially harmful and manipulative interference, which take such forms as the prohibition of subliminal commercial advertisements or the regulation of "fake news".

However, the essential question at the present time of rapid technological innovation is whether the law is adequate to guarantee the absence of similar manipulative practices in other sectors or related to other phenomena, such as neuromarketing, recommender systems or brain spyware. In other words, can the law safeguard the cognitive freedom of the mind as an essential part of a life of human dignity, or have we already entered a time in which "private thought" is an oxymoron? This question is of particular relevance for certain technologies now widely summarised as "artificial intelligence" (AI), which affect the mind through different means known as "subliminal priming", meaning "stimulation below the threshold of awareness that changes the probability of the later occurrence of related cognitive tasks".[2] In law and, notably, the enforcement of law, the issue of subliminal phenomena raises the paradoxical dilemma of how to detect the undetectable.

Trying to answer this paradox will require a fresh look at the role of law and regulation in protecting the mind from potentially harmful

DOI: 10.4324/9781003319436-1

and manipulative interference. It will first require a better coordination and greater consistency between different laws and legal disciplines. At the same time, it will call for a closer cooperation between legal science and other scientific areas, particularly neuroscience. In short, neuroscience matters greatly to law.[3] After all, neuroscience focuses on the brain and the mind, and it is from both these that law and normativity emanate.[4] What about the reverse, then? Does law also matter to neuroscience? If it does not, it clearly should. Here, it is the growing sophistication of AI, with its fundamental significance for our lives and the decisions we take, that mandates a closer surveillance of its impact on human existence and a serious legal debate centred on how best to regulate it in all its different varieties. In concrete terms, AI's growing sophistication may require us not only to regulate AI specifically but also to revisit some fundamental rights, like the right to freedom of thought and conscience, with a view to developing them into a coherent right to "mental privacy and cognitive liberty". At the same time, it calls for the adoption of entirely new legal concepts, or the evolutionary interpretation of existing legal concepts, in line with the progress made in the scientific understanding of the human mind. This is of particular importance given that the aim of AI itself is to understand the foundations and running mechanisms of the human mind and "trying to reproduce them artificially".[5]

In academic debates this trend can be seen in the growing interest in the link between law and neuroscience or in the transdisciplinary field of study called "neurolaw".[6] As AI is already having a major impact on society, which will become even greater with the growing intrusion of technology into the human brain, there is growing urgency for regulatory steps to be taken.[7] Thus far, these steps have been taken through initiatives to establish ethical principles for the adoption of socially beneficial AI. Among them, the five ethical principles for AI should be mentioned: *beneficence, non-maleficence, autonomy, justice* and *explicability.* [8] However, these central ethical principles for AI will not suffice in the long run, and they need to be matched with related legislative or regulatory efforts as, so far, there have been no adequate responses in concrete terms. This is why the European Commission's proposal for an Artificial Intelligence Act (AIA) for the European Union (EU), which was presented in April 2021, stands out as a major and comprehensive legislative effort to regulate artificial intelligence.[9] Although it is restricted to the territory of the EU, the proposal is likely to have effects beyond the EU's jurisdiction, in line with the EU's aspiration to be "a global leader in the development of secure, trustworthy and ethical Artificial Intelligence".[10] Given the scope of this proposed regulatory framework for AI, it is expected to mark "a defining moment in the history of AI, since it will ultimately lead to the first comprehensive legislative measure globally containing binding rules on AI".[11]

Generally, the AIA attempts to create a broad and comprehensive regulatory framework for AI. However, in the present book the principal focus will be on one specific aspect of AI, namely the potentially manipulative effects of AI systems. In this regard, the AIA is based on the consideration that although artificial intelligence has many beneficial uses, it "can also be misused and provide novel and powerful tools for manipulative, exploitative and social control practices".[12] Therefore, the Act proposes the prohibition of various manipulative practices, among which it specifically mentions the "use of an *AI system that deploys subliminal techniques beyond a person's consciousness*".[13]

This specific provision marks just one of many important aspects of AI, but also meets with considerable difficulties. First, it must be noted that the provision does not define or further explain the meaning of the concepts used, such as, notably, "subliminal technique" or "materially distort a person's behaviour". Second, these challenges include the problem of establishing absolute thresholds of conscious perception for each of the individual senses alone, as well as all of them together. As reflected in the notion of synaesthesia (lit. "to sense together" from "*syn* = together + *aisthēsis* = perception"),[14] the individual senses not only act in isolation but also mutually influence each other. It is imperative to ask whether such universal thresholds exist or whether the thresholds are subject to both inter- and intrapersonal variances. Third, the provision necessitates a sound understanding of what can be included in the category of so-called "subliminal AI systems". This technical question is exacerbated by the fact that the provision not only applies to existing technologies but also aims to embrace and forecast the nature of future technologies. This is why it is necessary to try to forecast what kind of AI systems deploying subliminal techniques are likely to be developed in the near future.

Addressing these difficulties also requires the due consideration of the wider implications for the EU's legal system as a whole, in parallel with the development of the related legal areas, like the individual senses function to form a more coherent whole. Last but not least, in line with the extraterritorial "Brussels effect" observed in the context of the General Data Protection Regulation (GDPR),[15] the proposed regulation for AI will also have wider territorial implications, which will also require more serious regulatory efforts to be taken at the global level. In early December 2021, the Council of Europe's Ad Hoc Committee on Artificial Intelligence (CAHAI) adopted the document entitled "Possible elements of a legal framework on artificial intelligence, based on the Council of Europe's standards on human rights, democracy and the rule of law", which outlines plans for an appropriate legal framework for AI for the Council of Europe which could enter into force in 2024.[16] This document is not available at the time of writing, but a preparatory report, unlike an earlier Declaration by the Committee of Ministers on the manipulative capabilities of algorithmic processes, does not mention subliminal techniques.[17] Given the Council of Europe's wider membership, it would have an even wider reach than the proposed AIA.

Therefore, the ideal global scenario would be the development of a comprehensive and legally binding standard-setting instrument on AI with a strong ethical basis, following-up on the Recommendation on the Ethics of Artificial Intelligence adopted by UNESCO in November 2021 in order both to protect and to promote human rights and human dignity.[18] More concretely, the UNESCO Recommendation also addresses the potential dangers of AI for the mind in the following words:

> Recognizing the profound and dynamic positive and negative impacts of artificial intelligence (AI) on societies, environment, ecosystems and human lives, *including the human mind*, in part because of the new ways in which its use influences human thinking, interaction and decision-making and affects education, human, social and natural sciences, culture, and communication and information.[19]

In words that are reminiscent of the UNESCO constitution, it can be freely stated that "since artificial intelligence systems begin in the minds of men, it is in the minds of men that the defences of human intelligence must be constructed".[20] It is also important to recall that UNESCO's predecessor was the International Commission for Intellectual Cooperation (ICIC), which was created in 1921 by the League of Nations.[21]

Similarly, the Organisation for Economic Co-operation and Development (OECD) has also adopted a recommendation on responsible innovation in neurotechnology, which warns of the range of unique ethical, legal, and societal questions raised by neurotechnology, as illustrated in the following extract:

> These questions include issues of (brain) data privacy, the prospects of human enhancement, the regulation and marketing of

> direct-to-consumer devices, the vulnerability of cognitive patterns for commercial or political manipulation, and further inequalities in use and access. Governance issues surrounding neurotechnology affect the entire innovation pipeline, from fundamental brain research, cognitive neuroscience, and other brain-inspired sciences to questions of commercialisation and marketing.[22]

At the same time, the recommendation recognises the "different cultural understandings of the brain and mind", which mean that "there may be diverse ways of putting responsible innovation into practice" and that "such diversity creates an opportunity for learning".[23]

In sum, although there is a wide consensus that AI must be regulated, so far there has been no comprehensive legislation adopted that specifically regulates the use of AI.[24] Nonetheless, it is also likely that there is no country on this planet that is not currently considering new strategies in the field of artificial intelligence. In this regard, the debates are certainly not limited to the EU, the US, China and Russia.[25] However, there is less awareness and prior legislative activity about the role of subliminal techniques used by AI systems. This is why the present book focuses on the role of the mind in general, and the effect of subliminal techniques on it in particular, in order to contribute to the debate by taking a closer look and paying wider attention.

In view of the above, the present book therefore sets out to make a critical exploration of the manifold legal and scientific challenges related to the proposed prohibition of subliminal techniques employed by AI and various related technologies. Following these introductory comments, Chapter 1 first presents a brief explanation of the AIA proposed by the EU, looking particularly at its purpose and context. It then analyses the relevant provision on the prohibition of the use of AI systems that deploy subliminal techniques. For a better understanding of the scope and relevance of the legal provision, the same chapter also presents several examples of AI systems that are already deploying, or are likely in the future to deploy, subliminal techniques.

Dedicated to the field of "subliminal psychology", Chapter 2 then turns to the specific question of subliminal perception as discussed in psychology, marketing and related scientific fields. It traces the beginnings of regulatory action that were prompted by novel findings in the field of motivational research, as reflected in the commonly known example of the screening of subliminal messages inducing cinema audiences to buy certain snacks and drinks. Following the outline of the hidden persuaders used by the advertising industry, the principal

European laws containing prohibitions on subliminal advertising are mentioned and briefly discussed. However, the overview is not limited to Europe and some further examples of legal cases involving subliminal messages, such as backward masking in music and the allegation that this can cause suicide or attempted suicide, are briefly presented.

Chapter 3 seeks to make a critical examination of the need for regulation of subliminal techniques used by AI systems by projecting some of the present developments into a wider future. The legal analysis also takes into account the wider ramifications, for other legal instruments and areas of law, of attempts to regulate techniques of subliminal perception. It touches upon the fundamental right to freedom of thought as the primary, but not the sole, fundamental right concerning matters of the mind. Inspired by the fields of semiotics and language as well as technology, the chapter closes with a more theoretical assessment of the need for law and legal education to adapt to the drastic changes in the regulatory environment. Using the term "legal synaesthesia", it draws on an analogy between the need for a greater "union of the senses", which is matched by the attempts of new technologies to enhance the perception of the senses through augmented reality devices, and the aim of achieving a greater coherence and consistency in law.

The Conclusion ends with an attempt to integrate the main findings on the relevance of, and necessity for, the regulation of AI, in general, and the prohibition of subliminal techniques, in particular.

Notes

1 Thomas St. Aquinas, *The 'Summa Theologica' of St. Thomas Aquinas* (New York: Benziger Brothers, 1915) 18.
2 Gary R. VandenBos (ed.), *APA Dictionary of Psychology*, 2nd ed. (Washington: American Psychological Association, 2015) 1044.
3 Antonio D'Aloia, "Law Challenged. Reasoning About Neuroscience and Law" in Antonio D'Aloia and Maria Chiara Errigo (eds.), *Neuroscience and Law: Complicated Crossings and New Perspectives* (Cham: Springer, 2020) 1–36, 1.
4 Michael S. Pardo and Dennis Patterson, *Minds, Brains, and Law: The Conceptual Foundations of Law and Neuroscience* (Oxford: Oxford University Press, 2013) xiii, and Rostam J. Neuwirth, "Law as Mnemonics: The Mind as the Prime Source of Normativity" (2008) 2(1) *European Journal of Legal Studies* 143–182, 144.
5 Pier Luigi Gentili, "The human sensory system as a collection of specialized fuzzifiers: A conceptual framework to inspire new artificial intelligent systems computing with words" (2014) 27 *Journal of Intelligent & Fuzzy Systems* 2137–2151, 2137.

6 Arian Petoft and Mahmoud Abbasi, "A Historical Overview of Law and Neuroscience: From the Emergence of Medico-Legal Discourses to Developed Neurolaw" (2019) 10(2) *Journal on European History of Law* 15–33, 15.
7 Eduardo Magrani, "New perspectives on ethics and the laws of artificial intelligence" (2019) 8(3) *Internet Policy Review* 1–19, 15.
8 Luciano Floridi and Josh Cowls, "A Unified Framework of Five Principles of AI in Society" (2019) 1.1 *Harvard Data Science Review* 1–15, 1; doi:10.1162/99608f92.8cd550d1.
9 European Commission, *Proposal for a Regulation Laying Down Harmonised Rules on Artificial Intelligence (Artificial Intelligence Act)*, COM (2021) 206 final (21 April 2021) [AIA].
10 European Council, *Special meeting of the European Council (1 and 2 October 2020) – Conclusions*, EUCO 13/20 (2 October 2020) para. 13.
11 Thomas Burri and Fredrik von Bothmer, "The New EU Legislation on Artificial Intelligence: A Primer" (22 April 2021); https://ssrn.com/abstract=3831424; see also Graham Greenleaf, "The 'Brussels effect' of the EU's 'AI Act' on data privacy outside Europe" (2021) 171 *Privacy Laws & Business International Report* 1–10, 2, Eduardo Gill-Pedro, "The Most Important Legislation Facing Humanity? The Proposed EU Regulation on Artificial Intelligence" (2021) 1 *Nordic Journal of European Law* iv–x, v, Armen Zh. Stepanyan, "European Artificial Intelligence Act: Should Russia Implement the Same?" (2021) 8(3) *Kutafin Law Review* 403–422, 403, Michael Veale and Frederik Zuiderveen Borgesius, "Demystifying the Draft EU Artificial Intelligence Act" (2021) 22(4) *Computer Law Review International* 97–112, and Vera Lúcia Raposo, "Ex machina: preliminary critical assessment of the European Draft Act on artificial intelligence" (2022) *International Journal of Law and Information Technology* 1–22; https://doi.org/10.1093/ijlit/eaac007.
12 Recital 15 AIA, *supra* note 9.
13 Art. 5(1) lit. a) AIA, *supra* note 9 [*Italics* added].
14 Richard E. Cytowic, "Synesthesia: Phenomenology and Neuropsychology: A Review of Current Knowledge" (1995) 2(10) *Psyche: An Interdisciplinary Journal of Research on Consciousness* 1–22, 1.
15 Regulation (EU) 2016/679 (General Data Protection Regulation), OJ L 119/1–88 (4 May 2016) [GDPR].
16 Council of Europe Ad Hoc Committee on Artificial Intelligence (CAHAI), "News: The CAHAI held its 6th and final plenary meeting" (2 December 2021); https://www.coe.int/en/web/artificial-intelligence/-/outcome-of-cahai-s-6th-plenary-meeting.
17 Council of Europe CAHAI Secretariat, "Towards Regulation of AI Systems" (December 2020); https://rm.coe.int/prems-107320-gbr-2018-compli-cahai-couv-texte-a4-bat-web/1680a0c17a and Council of Europe, Recital 8 of the *Declaration by the Committee of Ministers on the manipulative capabilities of algorithmic processes* (Adopted by the Committee of Ministers on 13 February 2019 at the 1337 meeting of the Ministers' Deputies); https://search.coe.int/cm/pages/result_details.aspx?ObjectId=090000168092dd4b.
18 UNESCO General Conference, *Draft Text of the Recommendation on the Ethics of Artificial Intelligence*, 41st session, Paris, 2021, 41 C/73 (22 November 2021); https://unesdoc.unesco.org/ark:/48223/pf0000378931.

19 Recital 1 of the UNESCO Recommendation on AI [*Italics* added], *ibid.*

20 Recital 1 of the Preamble of the Constitution of the United Nations Educational, Scientific and Cultural Organization, (16 November 1945), 4 U.N.T.S. 275.

21 Rostam J. Neuwirth, "The UNESCO Convention and Future Technologies: "A Journey to the Center of Cultural Law and Policymaking" in Lilian Hanania-Richieri and Anne-Thida Nodorom (eds.), *Diversity of Cultural Expressions in the Digital Era* (Buenos Aires: TESEO, 2016) 85–111, 102.

22 OECD, *Recommendation of the Council on Responsible Innovation in Neurotechnology*, OECD/LEGAL/0457 (Paris: OECD, 2021) 5.

23 *Ibid.*

24 Jascha Galaski, "AI Regulation: Present Situation and Future Possibilities", *Liberties (Civil Liberties Union for Europe)* (8 September 2021); https://www.liberties.eu/en/stories/ai-regulation/43740.

25 Anton Saveliev and Denis Zhurenkov, "Artificial intelligence and social responsibility: the case of the artificial intelligence strategies in the United States, Russia, and China" (2021) 50(3) *Kybernetes* 656–675 and Huw Roberts et al., "The Chinese approach to artificial intelligence: an analysis of policy, ethics, and regulation" (2021) 36 *AI & Society: Knowledge, Culture and Communication* 59–77.

1 The European Union's proposed Artificial Intelligence Act (AIA)

On 21 April 2021, the European Commission published its draft *Proposal for a Regulation Laying Down Harmonised Rules on Artificial Intelligence*, known in brief as the "Artificial Intelligence Act" (AIA).[1] This draft is part of a broader effort of the European Union (EU) proactively to regulate and direct the development of new technologies in the present and the future. In 2016, a first important step was taken with the adoption of the EU's General Data Protection Regulation (GDPR).[2] Aided by its extraterritorial effect,[3] the GDPR has been described as a "law with powerful impact across multiple jurisdictions and continents".[4] Because of the general interconnectedness of the underlying technologies and their continuing convergence, the same global impact can be expected from other planned regulatory projects such as the proposed Digital Markets Act (DMA),[5] the Digital Services Act (DSA),[6] and, notably, the AIA.

The AIA has proved to be a laudable effort, but a global initiative in a multilateral context would have been preferable or could be recommended as a complementary initiative. This would, in particular, have helped to mitigate the regulatory "paradox of our times", which states that "the collective issues we must grapple with are increasingly global and, yet, the means for addressing these are national and local, weak and incomplete".[7] However, in a context in which a coherent global legal order is non-existent or purely theoretical,[8] the EU's initiative must be welcomed, especially as it provides a basis for an urgently needed constructive dialogue on a matter of extreme and ubiquitous importance. Notwithstanding the positive contribution of the EU initiative, it still requires better alignment and coordination with other national (e.g. Chinese, Russian, US), regional (e.g. Council of Europe) as well as global (e.g. UNESCO) initiatives in the future.

DOI: 10.4324/9781003319436-2

A Background and context

In the relatively long history of AI and the law,[9] the present draft AIA was long in the making and was preceded by a process involving several preparatory documents, a public consultation, and an impact assessment. In April 2018, the European Commission presented a communication entitled "Artificial Intelligence for Europe", which was based on the approach that artificial intelligence is already part of our lives and not mere science fiction.[10] However, even then it argued that a solid European framework for AI was needed, because the "way we approach AI will define the world we live in".[11] Although this document did not mention the dangers of subliminal AI techniques, it generally recognised that, like every piece of technology or tool, "AI can be used to positive but also to malicious ends" and, as such, "generates new opportunities, it also poses challenges and risks, for example in the areas of safety and liability, security (criminal use or attacks), bias and discrimination".[12] In sum, the document concluded that there was a need to put the power of AI at the service of human progress.[13]

Only a few months later, the European Commission followed up with a more concrete coordinated plan on AI.[14] This plan also recognised that AI was already part of daily life but that it has the potential to be much bigger, which requires both "a well-functioning data ecosystem built on trust, data availability and infrastructure" and "a regulatory framework that is flexible enough to promote innovation while ensuring high levels of protection and safety".[15]

Subsequently, the trust element gained further momentum, and this led the European Commission to set up a High-Level Expert Group on AI, which in April 2019 presented its Ethics Guidelines for Trustworthy Artificial Intelligence. These guidelines stated that, for AI to be trustworthy, it needed to be (1) lawful (respecting all applicable laws and regulations, (2) ethical (respecting ethical principles and values), and (3) robust (both from a technical perspective and also taking into account the social environment).[16] The same day, another document aimed at building trust in human-centric AI was issued by the European Commission.[17] This document emphasised, under the heading of "technical robustness and safety", the need of AI systems to be reliable and secure enough "to be resilient against both overt attacks and more subtle attempts to manipulate data or algorithms themselves".[18] Thus it mentioned the dangers posed by manipulation, but only went as far as manipulation of data and algorithms and not manipulation of the human mind itself. Other important elements referenced were those of "human agency and oversight", "privacy and data governance", "transparency", "diversity, non-discrimination and fairness", "societal and environmental well-being", and "accountability".[19] Shortly after this, the High-Level Expert Group on AI published a set of recommendations for broader AI policy, which also stressed the need for an appropriate governance and regulatory framework for AI.[20]

Another comprehensive document that was issued before the actual proposal was presented was a report on the safety and liability implications of AI. This mainly focused on the technical aspects of safety, and recognised that, in addition to the opportunities that AI, the Internet of Things (IoT), and robotics can bring to the economy and society, they are also prone to "create a risk of harm to legally protected interests, both material and immaterial ones". The report noted, too, that "such harm occurring will increase as the field of applications widens".[21] As an accompaniment to these policy papers, the European Commission also ensured the participation of the wider public, by way of public consultations that were organised throughout the year 2020 both prior to and following the publication of a white paper on artificial intelligence in February 2020.[22] Finally, the proposed draft AIA was published on 21 April 2021 in parallel to the presentation of an impact assessment and another communication.[23]

Ultimately, the proposed AIA first and foremost seeks to regulate high-risk AI systems that are already used or are likely to be used in the near future. In this regard the proposal seeks consistency with existing EU legislation, such as, in particular, the EU Charter of Fundamental Rights, as well as secondary sources, such as GDPR and the Law Enforcement Directive.[24] In terms of its purpose, the AIA identifies the following specific objectives:

- ensure that AI systems placed on the Union market and used are safe and respect existing law on fundamental rights and Union values;
- ensure legal certainty to facilitate investment and innovation in AI;
- enhance governance and effective enforcement of existing law on fundamental rights and safety requirements applicable to AI systems;
- facilitate the development of a single market for lawful, safe, and trustworthy AI applications and prevent market fragmentation.[25]

Divided into ten Titles, the proposal first provides a list of useful definitions of the relevant concepts and clarifies the subject matter and scope of the new rules. Notably, it provides a definition of "artificial intelligence system" (AI system), which is useful, as the concept had previously been considered to be an essentially contested concept, with no definite legal understanding having crystallised.[26] The term had also been described as an oxymoron, a contradiction in terms, on several occasions.[27] It is in order "to ensure legal certainty, while providing the flexibility to accommodate future technological developments" that the AIA defines the term "AI system" as follows:

> (1) 'artificial intelligence system' (AI system) means software that is developed with one or more of the techniques and approaches listed in Annex I and can, for a given set of human-defined objectives, generate outputs such as content, predictions, recommendations, or decisions influencing the environments they interact with.[28]

In this regard Annex I lists the following AI techniques and approaches referred to in Article 1 AIA:

> (a) machine learning approaches, including supervised, unsupervised and reinforcement learning, using a wide variety of methods including deep learning;
> (b) logic- and knowledge-based approaches, including knowledge representation, inductive (logic) programming, knowledge bases, inference and deductive engines, (symbolic) reasoning, and expert systems;
> (c) statistical approaches, Bayesian estimation, search and optimisation methods.[29]

It is important to highlight that this listing of different techniques is not an entirely static definition, and a dynamic regulatory tool has been integrated into the Act "in order to update that list to market and technological developments on the basis of characteristics that are similar to the techniques and approaches".[30] This marks an important feature in a time of rapid technological innovation, when it is difficult for law to "preserve its integrity over time, while managing to address the newly emerging circumstances that continually arise throughout our history".[31]

It is in the following Title II that a list of prohibited AI practices is established. Following a risk-based approach, the Act differentiates between uses of AI that create (i) an unacceptable risk, (ii) a high risk, and (iii) a low or minimal risk. In broad terms, the list includes, first, all those AI systems whose use is considered unacceptable as contravening Union values. Among these it specifically addresses, first, those "practices that have a significant potential to manipulate persons through subliminal techniques beyond their consciousness".[32] Second, it mentions practices that "exploit vulnerabilities of specific vulnerable groups such as children or persons with disabilities in order to materially distort their behaviour in a manner that is likely to cause them or another person psychological or physical harm".[33]

Title III covers AI systems that create a high risk to the health and safety or fundamental rights of natural persons. For these systems, the AIA foresees numerous measures, which include, for instance, certain mandatory requirements, the establishment of a risk management system, and an ex ante conformity assessment procedure for these high risk AI systems prior to them being placed on the market or put into service.[34]

Through Title IV, several transparency obligations are introduced, and these will notably apply to those systems that "(i) interact with humans, (ii) are used to detect emotions or determine association with (social) categories based on biometric data, or (iii) generate or manipulate content ('deep fakes')".[35]

Title V contains several measures to support innovation "to create a legal framework that is innovation-friendly, future-proof and resilient to disruption".[36] These include so-called "regulatory sandboxes", which are used to "foster AI innovation by establishing a controlled experimentation and testing environment in the development and pre-marketing phase".[37]

The following Titles VI, VII, and VIII contain rules regarding the governance and implementation of the rules between the Union and its Member States.

The penultimate Title IX encourages the creation of codes of conduct, which aim to encourage providers of AI systems that are not high-risk to apply the mandatory requirements for high-risk AI systems in a voluntary manner by establishing a suitable framework governing them.[38] It stipulates that these codes can be drawn up by individual providers of AI systems, by organisations representing them, or by both, and that they should also involve users and any interested stakeholders and their representative organisations.

The remaining Titles X, XI and XII contain the final provisions that round up the proposed new regulatory EU framework for AI. They include a confidentiality requirement by the authorities for the information and data obtained in carrying out their tasks and activities, as well as penalties applicable to infringements of the regulation.[39] The penalties are exclusively pecuniary fines, counted in terms of either a lump sum or a percentage of a company's total worldwide annual turnover for the preceding financial year, but they should be effective, proportionate, and dissuasive. These provisions also set up a committee procedure (Title XI) and contain a list of legislative acts to be amended (Title XII).

As the central focus of the present book is those AI practices that have a significant potential to manipulate persons through subliminal techniques, it is necessary to take a closer look at the relevant provisions.

B The prohibition of AI systems deploying subliminal techniques

The AIA thus proposes to prohibit AI systems that have the potential to manipulate persons by deploying subliminal techniques. This prohibition marks an essential, and probably the most fundamental, element of the proposed regulation, which – regardless of possible amendments made in the ongoing legislative process[40] – must be maintained in essence and should also be considered in other jurisdictions. One reason is that rapid developments in the field of artificial intelligence have been mentioned as posing serious threats to society and democracy, particularly based on their ability to manipulate people.[41] In this regard it is noteworthy that several experiments have confirmed the impact of subliminal messages on political behaviour, as follows:

> Together, results across three studies show that subliminal presentation of a national flag can bring about significant changes not only in a citizen's expressed political opinions within an experimental setting but also in their 'real-life' overt political behavior, perhaps the most significant political behavior of all, voting, temporally and contextually distant from the experiment.[42]

Equally, confirming the power of words, several studies support the conclusion that the subliminal exposure of individuals to hostile words and other messages results in significantly more aggressive behaviour.[43] The current and future threats for democracy posed by AI, and the related means of digital manipulation, have already been identified in the context of elections.[44] Even for search engines alone, studies have found that the rankings of internet queries have considerable effects on consumer behaviour and businesses.[45] The same effect of search engine power to manipulate internet search results has been shown to have an influential impact on voter behaviour and elections.[46] Search engines do not even use subliminal techniques per se unless a hidden algorithm can be characterised as such. For this reason, the prohibition of subliminal techniques is important and may allow the threats of AI to be separated from its beneficial effects for democracy.[47]

While the Act defines the notion of AI itself, it merely mentions "subliminal techniques" without further specifying the meaning of this and related terms such as "material distortion of a person's behaviour". Most preparatory documents mention various risks of AI, including those having an impact on the mind and behaviour. For instance, a study supporting the impact assessment of the AIA stresses the importance of a human-centric approach to AI for the following reasons:

> The need for a human-centric approach to AI has been stated by the European Commission, as well as by several other institutions and private organisations. In executing tasks, AI can be used to exert a significant impact on human agency, *including triggering cognitive manipulation through 'dark patterns' and interaction with sub-conscious processes*; generating addiction on the side of the end-user; hyper-nudging individuals towards specific purchasing decisions (e.g. recommendation systems) or political opinions (Cambridge Analytica).[48]

The mention of "dark patterns" in this context is interesting, as this is another broader but perhaps synonymous term for manipulative practices that use subliminal techniques to target the mind. The example of dark patterns that is provided is the manipulation of a user interface by "embedding subliminal stimuli to influence and encourage users to purchase more products (unethical marketing)".[49] It has been noted that dark patterns are increasingly used in a variety of products worldwide. These dark patterns can be simply defined as "deceptive elements that are intentionally crafted to make the users do actions that they wouldn't do otherwise".[50] These dark pattern practices have been found not only to be anticompetitive in effect but also to pose more serious risks, as outlined in the following paragraph:

> With attention and data, platforms can exploit their *users' cognitive vulnerabilities* in the form of "*dark patterns,*" which are subtle design choices meant to guide individuals towards behaviors sought by the platform, as well as *other forms of digital manipulation*. Digital manipulation is effective because it makes one's

> actions – such as the sharing of photos, messages, geolocation, and contacts – *appear like an exercise of free will.* This threatens an underexplored aspect of privacy called "*decisional privacy,*" referring to *one's ability to make choices free of coercion.*[51]

Evidence that this threat to both decisional and personal privacy may be caused by dark patterns or similar design tricks is found in the so-called "privacy paradox". This paradox describes the obvious "inconsistencies between our stated privacy preferences and our actual disclosure behaviour".[52]

However, the first explicit use of the term "subliminal techniques" appears to be in the proposal for the AIA itself, as well as the so-called "Impact Assessment", both of which were made available on 21 April 2021. The Impact Assessment recognises the potential misuse of AI for manipulation and the harmful effects of this on users, and more concretely states as follows:

> Evidence suggests that AI supported products or services (toys, personal assistants etc.) can be *intentionally designed or used in ways that appeal to the subliminal perception of individuals, thus causing them to take decisions that are beyond their cognitive capacities.* Even if the techniques used are not subliminal, for certain categories of vulnerable subjects, in particular children, these might have the same adverse manipulative effects if their mental infirmity, age or credulity are exploited in harmful ways.[53]

It is interesting to note that the reference to the subliminal perception of the individual refers to a document dated 2016 issued by the White House Office of Science and Technology Policy, which only contains a single reference to subliminal control in the following passage:

> Also, in 5 years Virtual Reality is going to be in millions of homes across the U.S. As online communications become more sensory, autonomous programs as mentioned above, may be capable of *subliminal control* through online video, rss feeds, social media, or gaming. This could create extreme reactions from citizens that might cause them to initiate or weaponized against virtual threats that are tactical to a programs initiative.[54]

Further on, the Impact Assessment highlights the need for greater protection against "certain manipulative and exploitative AI systems", and to this end justifies the prohibition of subliminal techniques by reference to "the increasing power of algorithms to subliminally influence human choices and important decisions interfering with human agency and the principle of personal autonomy".[55]

In sum, it is not clear how the specific term "subliminal techniques" was added to the text of the AIA, but it can be said to have emerged from a combination of concerns from the technological, psychological, and legal sides. For this reason, the term "subliminal techniques" will be crucial in the enforcement of the prohibition once it enters into force. Therefore, it is important to interpret its meaning, which requires us first to take a closer look at the relevant passages in the regulation.

The first mention of "subliminal" is in the Preamble, which explains the underlying reasons for the prohibition in the following way: "The placing on the market, putting into service or use of certain AI systems intended to distort human behaviour, whereby physical or psychological harms are likely to occur, should be forbidden".[56] The Preamble goes on to explain the reason for this, which is that such AI systems deploy subliminal components that individuals cannot perceive. It is the fact that the thing cannot be perceived that makes it easier to manipulate a person's behaviour. Likewise, the Preamble states that the manipulation of human behaviour has to be carried out with "the intention to materially distort the behaviour of a person and in a manner that causes or is likely to cause harm to that or another person".[57]

These reasons are then translated into the substantive rule, which formulates the prohibition in the following words:

> Article 5 AIA
>
> 1. The following artificial intelligence practices shall be prohibited:
> (a) the placing on the market, putting into service or use of an *AI system that deploys subliminal techniques beyond a person's consciousness* in order to materially distort a person's behaviour in a manner that causes or is likely to cause that person or another person physical or psychological harm; […].[58]

The crucial element in the prohibition is that it involves an AI system that "deploys subliminal techniques beyond a person's consciousness". In this phrase, the terms "subliminal", "techniques" and "consciousness" are key to the interpretation of the said article, but – unlike the term AI – none of them is further clarified in the text of the proposal.

To begin with "subliminal", this word derives from the Latin "*sub*" and *"limen,-inis*", and etymologically means "below the threshold of consciousness".[59] Subliminal thus refers to the sensory threshold separating the conscious from the subconscious perception, and therefore also requires an understanding of the term consciousness. A sensory threshold has been defined as "the stimulus level that supports a certain probability of making a particular decision".[60] This is, first of all, important for the later discussion of the right to freedom of thought and conscience, which raises the question of how consciousness and conscience relate to each other as part of the assessment of whether the prohibition on meddling with a person's consciousness is backed by the right to the freedom of conscience. Although both terms are used in various scientific disciplines and are also confused, it is safe to assert that both "conscience and consciousness are part of a system of information that governs our experience and decision making process".[61] Second, this question is also relevant for the field of AI, which aims to reproduce human intelligence artificially by, for instance, giving robots consciousness and conscience. It is in this context that a useful explanation of the terms consciousness and conscience has been given as follows:

> Consciousness and conscience are related in various ways. They both have the same Latin root derived of *con* = with and *scientia* = knowledge. In human evolution, consciousness was a precondition for conscience. First, humans developed a consciousness, becoming aware of their existence and their actions, and why they performed them. Later, they developed a conscience telling them whether their actions were right or wrong.[62]

This quote clearly helps to establish both a logical order in the relationship and the combined relevance of the two concepts for human existence and decision-making. It seems, however, that conscience, in order to perform its task, is preconditioned upon the existence of consciousness. This results from the following explanation:

> "Consciousness" is the function of the human mind that receives and processes information, crystallizes it and then stores it or rejects it with the help of the following:
>
> 1 The five senses
> 2 The reasoning ability of the mind
> 3 Imagination and emotion
> 4 Memory

> The five senses enable the mind to receive information, then imagination and emotion process it, reason judges it, and memory stores or rejects it.[63]

This marks a useful explanation of the complexity of the cognitive process underlying consciousness, although the order of the cognitive steps and the taxonomy of the senses, especially the limitation to five senses, is problematic, as will become obvious in the later discussion of synaesthesia, a state of mind "in which stimulation of one sense generates a simultaneous sensation in another".[64]

This description gives a good summary of the definition of consciousness as "the phenomenon of personal, subjective experience", which is "is sensory, remembered, or imagined in nature and interacts with environment and physiological states so as to produce changes in the state or aspects of subjective experience".[65] In line with humans' traditional dualistic way of thinking,[66] the remaining question could be regarded as the antonym of the first, namely a "subconscious" or an "unconscious" state of subjective experience. Given that subconscious is defined as "below or out of consciousness, as in thought or other mental processes occurring without the knowledge of the thinker", it seems that it has to be given preference over "unconscious", which more generally refers to "any process or content of the mind of which the individual is not aware at a particular moment in time".[67]

In this regard, more information regarding the meaning attached to the term "subliminal" is needed and, most of all, research needs to continue.[68] If this is not done, it may give rise to the confusion that characterises the controversy about the efficiency of subliminal techniques, as reflected in the following paragraph:

> Thus, subliminal stimuli—because they arc outside a human's ability to perceive them—can have no effect on humans. When people use the term *subliminal advertising effects*, what they really mean is "unconscious effects of advertising." This unconscious influence is a powerful effect. In fact, advertisers depend on it; that is why they spend hundreds of millions of dollars on ad campaigns to embed their ads in highly cluttered environments—like in commercial pods on TV and radio, pages of newspapers and magazines, and websites.[69]

This explains the need to ask whether the opposition of subliminal and supraliminal perception is accurate, especially when it is combined with that of subconscious and conscious perception. The reason is that it leaves unanswered the question of whether there is a threshold which is "beyond our consciousness". This is essential in the context of the AIA, which somewhat misleadingly speaks about "subliminal techniques *beyond* a person's consciousness". Perception beyond our consciousness should instead be termed "paraliminal perception", given that "*para*" means "beyond". Paraliminal perception could then denote the threshold for information that lies beyond our sensory abilities or within our sensory abilities but beyond the cognitive abilities of the mind to detect. This raises the question of whether it is linguistically necessary to distinguish the abilities of the senses from those of the brain. In other words, do we see with the mind's eye or with the human eye?[70] In any event, it appears that a more integrated approach is more suitable for regulatory purposes. This seems to be more adequate, given the following observation:

> It is believed that images in ultraviolet light or other shades on the light spectrum that fall just below or above the range of human sight can influence someone. Just because one's eyes don't see the light does not mean that they cannot understand it at some level in the brain. The brain has the ability to perceive things far beyond the scope that our conscious minds perceive.[71]

A broader brain-based approach also seems more in line with the general definition of "subliminal" to refer to "*stimuli below the limen or threshold of conscious perception*".[72] Still, as the emphasis of subliminal is on "below" (Latin "*sub*") and not "beyond", it could be argued that, strictly speaking, the regulation would have been correct to state "subliminal techniques *below* and not *beyond* a person's consciousness". This of course depends on whether there also exists a threshold beyond one's consciousness, which should then be termed "paraliminal perception", as "*para*" means "beyond". The difference is that, in the first case, information is received but not noticed, whereas, in the second case, the information appears to be impossible or out of reach. The term "beyond" would instead be suitable for paranormal or extrasensory modes of perception, manifest in phenomena described as precognition, retrocausality, intuition, or near-death experiences.[73] It is safe to state, given that there exist several inconsistent yet independently plausible theses about it, that consciousness thus remains paradoxical in many ways.[74]

Another more suitable term could be "transliminal perception", which is used to refer to stimuli crossing (*trans*) thresholds (*limines*) "into or out of consciousness", both below and above our ordinary level of consciousness.[75] This would also reflect the reality that both subliminal and supraliminal cognition influences our behaviour, including ethical decision-making.[76] An approach using transliminal in its terminology would also be in line with exceptional experiences in combination with the condition known as synaesthesia, which describes different forms of simultaneous interactions between the individual senses.[77] A greater involvement of all the senses is already aimed at in the economy and, notably, in multisensory marketing practices. It may also assume greater importance in the future evolution of the senses.

For the present context, the main challenge is to find the best possible terminology to describe manipulative and at the same time harmful practices. In relation to the issue of subliminal perception, it has been stated that there is no obstacle to the coherent conceptualisation of the term but that "a major source of the persistent controversy revolves around the proliferation of competing terminology and lack of clarification concerning what the terms precisely mean, which leads to competing claims and apparent contradictions within the literature".[78] Similar observations can be made about the term "subliminal techniques" and its synonymous relationship to "dark patterns" or "hidden persuaders". For the proposed prohibition of AI systems using such practices, the essential point is that the person is unable to become aware of the stimulus received, regardless of whether it is below or beyond their consciousness. Unfortunately, it is not scientifically clear what constitutes a subliminal and what a supraliminal stimulus. The principal question in this regard is to consider what precisely constitutes the particular threshold, that is, where the line between being aware and being unaware is being drawn, or even whether it is possible or necessary to draw such a line. This is why the present book considers it essential to continue the search for the optimal choice of terminology, in line with ongoing as well as future directions of scientific research. One of these related questions is addressed by psychophysics, the branch of science that studies, inter alia, the thresholds of sensible perception. These specific thresholds matter, first, for each of the senses alone, and, second, for the interaction of all the senses collectively. This particular aspect will be addressed in Chapter 2.C in the context of the individual senses and their mutual interaction in synaesthesia.

As a next step, once a subliminal practice has been identified, it is important to look at the requirement "*in order to materially distort a person's behaviour*". This requirement depends upon the extent to which "subliminal techniques" can be scientifically proven to have some kind of measurable impact on human behaviour. In this regard, the term "subliminal" has been defined as "of or relating to stimuli to which the individual responds but of which the individual is not conscious".[79] By including a reference to a response, this definition implicitly seems to support the hypothesis that subliminal information has an effect – an issue that will be revisited in greater detail in Chapter 3 below. Hence, once a subliminal practice has been identified, it is necessary to look at whether it can materially distort a person's behaviour. Although the adverb "materially" has a double meaning, in that it can mean "substantially" or "significantly" or can refer to some kind of material ("matter from which a thing is made"), the text is likely to refer to the former meaning in the present context.[80] This because the next criterion is the ability to cause physical or psychological harm, which includes not only physical but also other non-tangible forms of harm. In this regard, harm should be interpreted in a holistic and non-dualistic way that is reminiscent of the World Health Organization's comprehensive definition of "health" as "a state of complete physical, mental and social well-being and not merely the absence of disease or infirmity".[81]

Further support for this assertion can be obtained from tort law in combination with neuroscience and new technologies, such as functional magnetic resonance imaging (fMRI).[82] The term "fMRI" refers to "a non-invasive method for studying the functional anatomy of the human brain".[83] Since it can be applied in a wide range of domains and has already been applied in domains that are "highly diverse, ranging from language comprehension or short-term memory to personality traits, political behavior, or aesthetic judgment", fMRI raises key ethical questions with regard to the possible implications and applications of its research.[84] In this regard it has already been stated that "greater clarity and certainty about the status of emotions in the legal framework are needed to provide a robust system of protection to the consumer where her emotions are at stake".[85] This must also include subliminal effects on emotions since, even in 1992, there were two studies confirming that subliminal stimuli were capable of affecting people's emotions and attitudes towards others.[86] Unfortunately for our emotional well-being, another study seems to confirm that even subliminal "negative stimuli enjoy preferential access to perceptual processing".[87] This may help to explain the prevalent use of negative information, sensationalism and violence in news reporting, entertainment, advertising and social media.[88] More generally, the planned prohibition should still be accompanied by a wider debate on whether subliminal techniques may be capable not only of "mesmerizing the minds of the masses" but also of shaping public opinion and the resulting realities for societies around the world.[89]

In this regard, the AIA was considered to be "under-protective", and the suggestion was made to widen the scope of harms from merely physical and psychological harms to other significant and potentially more serious harms, such as "financial and economic harms, cultural harms, harms of recognition and autonomy harms, but also collective and societal harms".[90] In this regard, considerations of "cumulative harms", which refer to "a product which does cumulative damage as more units are consumed", should also be included.[91] This matters especially for certain products and practices covered by the present regulation, as has been pointed out:

> In real life, harm can accumulate without a single event tripping a threshold of seriousness, leaving it difficult to prove. These 'cumulative' harms are reinforced over time by their impact on individuals' environments, with hyperpersonalisation, engagement and 'dwell' metrics and impact on children often called out in this regard.[92]

The practical problems of proving cumulative subliminal causes of harm are exemplified in a decision rendered by the Advertising Standards Authority of the United Kingdom. In the case, three complainants challenged whether the implication in an advertisement suggesting that electromagnetic radiation and associated products posed a risk to health, such as damage to the immune system, electrosensitivity, skin disorders, cancer risks, headaches, memory loss, and so on, was misleading and could be substantiated.[93] In its decision the authority ruled in favour of the claimants and found that the ad constituted misleading advertising, because the claims of a large part of the general population being subliminally electrosensitive and bio-effects of electromagnetic exposure being cumulative were not supported by robust scientific evidence.[94] This matter exemplifies the combined scientific and legal problems of establishing causality of harms that may accumulate over time and are experienced below the normal levels of awareness.[95] The problem is well-known in scientific studies trying to establish causal links between mental health problems or the ideation of suicides and the use of media,[96] social media,[97] or the internet.[98]

By the same token, and a crucial point in the quest for an adequate model of future societies,[99] another comment raises the issue that AI applications may cause only negligible harms to individuals but significant "societal-level harms" collectively. This can be exemplified as follows:

> For example, a political marketing application may reduce a person's desire to vote by a small amount. At an individual level, the impact of this application may not be considered an infringement of fundamental rights, but collectively, the effect may be large enough to change an election result.[100]

This is also linked to other outcomes of such manipulations, such as those achieved through "automation bias" or "algorithmic bias".[101] Here too it has been argued that the AIA offers little protection, particularly with regard to affective computing and algorithmic manipulation.[102] Research has shown how such techniques can create biases of all kinds by repeatedly and specifically exposing persons to biased information.[103]

In these cases the cumulative effect is based on a collective of individuals. Such societal-level harms not only should be included but also call into question the efficiency and proportionality of the planned penalties. To formulate this differently, how would the effect of a rigged election be valued in financial terms, and how could such danger be averted, as a company could be set up only to achieve this effect, as we were reminded in the Cambridge Analytica scandal.[104] Overall, even if this issue cannot be solved on the sole basis of the AIA, it should lead to further discussions about updates to the tort and related systems (e.g. product liability),[105] the question of common ownership (i.e. concentration in and across different industries),[106] and the concept of causation (in line with analogous experiences of climate change issues).[107]

As early as the 1980s, new media techniques caused concern and invited a search for a "subliminal tort", as described in the following:

> The discovery of new media techniques for the modification of the behavior of persons without their awareness raises the specter of a society whose freedom has become an illusion. No clear regulatory or common law prohibitions exist against most of these techniques. Nevertheless, a clear movement of the law indicates a growing sensitivity to the concept and the pervasiveness of subliminal influences, and to the companion notion that such influences are *prima facie* offensive.[108]

For both the present AIA as well as any future tort system that is sensitive to subtle cumulative harms, the principal problem remains the establishment of reliable evidence about the use of a subliminal technique and causality in terms of the harm caused. Addressing this problem will also require more inputs from neuroscientists to the legal debate generally and to adjudication in particular.[109] Unfortunately, in these cases the legal decision is often rendered more difficult by the paradox of scientific authority, which states that "the cases in which scientific advice is asked most urgently are those in which the authority of science is questioned most thoroughly".[110]

In addition to the general difficulties with the scientific reality of causation, there are also several concerns about the question of "subliminal thresholds". Addressing these, however, first requires a closer look at the nature of present and future AI practices that may affect subliminal levels of perception. After that, light will be cast on the physiology of human perception and on what subliminal means for the individual senses and for all of them together.

C The scope and nature of AI systems with subliminal aspects

In order to assess both the justifiability and the feasibility of a legal prohibition on subliminal techniques, it is also important to understand what factual situations it may cover, in terms of both present and future technologies. In this regard, when the proposal was presented, the competent Commissioner cited the example of "a toy that uses voice assistance to manipulate a child into doing something dangerous".[111] This example, however, relates instead to the following paragraph in Article 5(1)(b), which prohibits AI systems that exploit "the vulnerabilities of a specific group of persons due to their age, physical or mental disability". Currently, it is therefore difficult to point to or even conceive of a concrete AI system that deploys subliminal techniques. Therefore, a good starting point is provided by the field of commercial advertisement, which has also been subject to the prohibition of such techniques for a long time, as will be discussed below.

In advertising, AI can, first, be expected to help to improve efficiency and realise the expected outcomes, particularly through specifically targeted advertisements and when combined with big data, machine learning, and neuroscience.[112] Labelled as a new scientific area, neuromarketing has been defined as the area that "deals with the subliminal reaction of consumers in connection with marketing materials such as brands, products, and product lines".[113] There are already a large number of new tools and technologies used to study consumer behaviour and the decision-making process in marketing, including electroencephalography (EEG), eye tracking (ET), fMRI, and the Internet of Everything (IoE).[114] Generally, AI, notably through machine learning, is said to enhance the performance of human beings by making them more efficient and productive.[115] Eye-tracking technology is a biometric tool that is already widely used in various commercial and research applications, such as computer gaming, education, entertainment, health, neuromarketing, and psychology. Recent eye-tracking and software simulation experiments have also revealed aspects of subliminal reality and our unconscious interactions with the environment.[116] In another study it was found that ambient persuasive technology, providing both supraliminal and subliminal feedback to users of household appliances, had an effect on the user's energy consumption. The most important finding, though, was that persuasive technology can persuade the user without receiving her/his conscious attention and that there are ethical concerns about subliminal information that require that "interventions that go beyond the control of the receiver should be regulated carefully".[117] Saving energy undoubtedly constitutes a more positive scenario, but the same techniques could also be used for negative or harmful effects. This is reflected in various paradoxes, such as those of "progress"[118] or of the "internet"[119], where it is the use that swings the pendulum towards there being positive or negative effects.[120]

The initial neutrality of new technologies can also be exemplified by recommender systems, which are already widely used by, for instance, search engines. The goal of recommender systems was defined as "to generate meaningful recommendations to a collection of users for items or products that might interest them".[121] In a time of internet infoglut, this seems a useful aspect, which has been described by saying that recommender systems have the ability "to offer relevant information in myriad settings, basically dealing with situations where an abundance of information makes it hard to detect and select what is required in a specific situation, or with situations where information itself cannot be accessed".[122] At the same time, they operate in the sphere of persuasion, which makes them prone to being used to manipulate targeted individuals, for instance via "spamdexing" or webmasters' practice of using "indexing terms that are completely irrelevant to actual Web page content in order to gain hits from searches on those topics".[123] Because of the many inherent dangers, recommender systems have also been identified as "traps" akin to those used for animals.[124] They have also been found to lead to forms of the subliminal manipulation described earlier as "dark patterns".[125] Dark patterns have also been said to manifest themselves "as induced states of 'non-action' or 'anti-action' – consider the absence of opt-out conditions, the struggle to unsubscribe, the preselected checkboxes and other defaults designed to hold decision making in suspense".[126] Just when trying to book a hotel room, many have already experienced such suspense because of messages reading "only 2 rooms left on our site" or "3 other persons looked for your dates in the last 10 minutes". It has also been shown that a simple subliminal technique, namely the showing of hotel videos embedded with a smiling face emoji as a subliminal message, can significantly affect consumers' selection of hotels.[127] In other words, recommender systems can also subconsciously put us in a situation from which there is no escape. Overall, neuromarketing and other neuroscience techniques share with other technologies the fact that their use generally gives rise to ethical concerns and that there are potential misuses.[128]

The same paradox also applies to algorithms in general, which are said to increasingly "know more about us than we ourselves can possibly do".[129] In someone else's hands, these powerful tools have a great influence over people's minds, an influence that can be variably and selectively used for positive and negative purposes. It is already a fact that these algorithms not only influence our decisions, but are also used in a great many areas in which they shape decisions that are beyond our control but affect our lives. The fact that they act in secrecy makes them especially prone to reach subliminal levels, which is why the following has also been stated: "Secrecy is approaching critical mass, and we are in the dark about crucial decisions. Greater openness is imperative."[130]

An example of this danger can be illustrated by the effects of so-called "automatic gender recognition" (AGR) systems when they are used for targeted advertising. These systems were found to be at risk of perpetuating gender stereotypes "by giving subliminal messages regarding artifacts that men versus women should use".[131] This kind of manipulative practice known from the advertisement sector, however, can also be used for and by the military sector. As another sector that operates in great secrecy, it is likely to use various security and military applications of AI. Various manipulation risks associated with neurotechnology have been identified, and it has been concluded that "the future sophistication and misuse of these techniques by malevolent actors may generate unprecedented opportunities for mental manipulation and brain-washing".[132] For military applications of neurotechnology, at present, three areas have been singled out, namely brain–computer interfaces (BCIs), neurotechnologies for warfighter enhancement (e.g. transcranial electric stimulation technology), and neurotechnological systems for deception, detection, and interrogation.[133]

BCIs in particular are becoming more sophisticated and are likely to prove a serious challenge in terms of being technical means for the direct and indirect manipulation of the mind. It has already been stated that "BCIs are moving beyond siloed research labs to explore new use-cases ranging from the arts and rehabilitation to gaming and augmented reality", and that the "[A]ccessibility, adaptability, and transparency of BCI tools and the data they collect will likely impact how we collectively navigate a new digital age".[134]

In this regard, subliminal techniques in AI can potentially be applied not only to improve human–computer interaction but also to make humans more productive.[135] For instance, these techniques can be applied to persuasive "social robots" and similar agents to allow them "to serve as personal, organizational, and public assistants as, for instance, diet coaches, teacher's aides, and emergency respondents".[136] In another field of application, AI has been used to recognise the importance of argumentation based on body language by making "persuasive cues visible to demonstrate the importance of the persuasive power of body-language-based argumentation".[137] Obviously, the same technologies can be used for desirable and for undesirable purposes, a frequently encountered paradoxical ambiguity that is reminiscent of the use of AI on the one hand to detect but on the other to create "fake news" or "deep fakes".[138]

Thus the same techniques can also be used with the intention of harming users. There already exist various technologies that can be used for subliminal suggestions and mind control. A good example is provided by so-called "brain spyware", a term which describes "software intentionally designed to detect private information".[139] This technology has been demonstrated in the lab to illustrate how

> brain hackers can deduce private information such as banking information, recognized faces, PIN numbers, location of residency and month of birth from the brains of BCI users by showing them visual stimuli and using a machine learning model to detect familiar information based on the brain's response.[140]

It is even more worrying that these attacks can be carried out subliminally, that is, in a way that is below the target's conscious perception.[141] By the same token, some seemingly harmless BCI and other subliminal devices targeting the different senses, such as wearable health devices used to track fitness or sleep, even if intended to "facilitate memory consolidation for learning purposes, enhance mood and wellbeing or even improve people's experience while communicating at a distance",[142] could still be misused to manipulate the users' minds without their awareness.

The brain can also be hacked while a person is asleep. Given that everyone needs to, and does, sleep, it is also generally accepted that everyone dreams.[143] Even though there are many questions that evade our understanding of sleep and dreams, we know that we continue to process information during sleep and even that sensory processing continues during sleep.[144] The fact that information processing continues during sleep means that it must be possible actively to influence or manipulate our brain and behaviour while we are asleep. One such form of influence has been known since ancient times by the term "dream incubation", which refers to "the practices, rituals, techniques and efforts that an individual applies to intentionally evoke helpful dreams".[145] More recently, there have been descriptions of a similar kind of manipulation using technology and known "dream-hacking techniques", which are said to be able not only to help us create, heal and have fun, but also to become tools of commercial manipulation.[146] Experiments have been conducted that confirm that "presenting the spoken name of a familiar, valued snack item during midday nap significantly improves the preference for that item relative to items not externally cued".[147] More subtle techniques, such as a "dream incubation device", can be used for "sleep hacking" in order carefully to manipulate a person to one of two very different, namely beneficial and harmful, ends. The core question in this regard is whether such effects on sleeping persons can be achieved using both sub- and supraliminal techniques affecting one or more senses. As experiments confirm that subliminal stimuli during wake time can affect sleep,[148] there seems to be no reason why they cannot also be effective during sleep. From a regulatory perspective, it would thus be interesting if any such technique deployed during sleep time becomes by definition a subliminal one, as the person can hardly be aware of any information while they are asleep.[149]

Still, more serious challenges than those we already know about will come from the creative combination of various existing and future AI systems, combining subliminal, supraliminal and BCI techniques as well as other devices.[150] For instance, BCI in the form of "affective computing" may give technology access not only to emotions but – possibly reinforced by rapid progress in the development of wearable health devices[151] – to our innermost thoughts and feelings too. Affective computing has been said to enable technology "to tap into someone's feelings or emotions", which gives it much promise in future applications and, as a result, gives rise to many concerns in areas including ethics, privacy and cost-effectiveness.[152] The same concerns were also expressed about the implementation of AI in clinical practice, which constitutes a promising area that "rapidly evolves together with the other modern fields of precision medicine, genomics and teleconsultation".[153] In sum, the prospect of AI, IoT, robots, and wearable and other health devices such as electronic medicine dispensers or anxiety reduction programs that play subliminal messages during the night is an important reminder that we should reflect on what sort of future is desirable. It has been said that this, particularly for mental health educators, researchers, and practitioners, requires a deeper reflection "on key ethical, cultural, social and political implications of the virtual information age".[154]

By way of a brief summary, existing and future BCIs and other technologies will further erode the distinctions not only between artificial and human intelligence or humans and machines but also between control by the mind and the machine and control by oneself or by someone else. The same applies to the military usage of AI in such things as autonomous weapons systems, for which "AI has the potential to support analysis by actors ranging from top-level political decision-makers all the way down to infantry soldiers in the field".[155] Generally, the autonomy of AI systems threatens the paradigm that the rule of law is based on human agency.[156] At the same time, human autonomy is also a multi-layered process in which many actions are performed in a subliminal manner, which further underlines the necessity of regulating subliminal techniques.[157]

Generally, numerous examples confirm that AI is a dual-use area of technology. This means that AI, like other dual-use products, has the potential for both a civilian and a military use, and the lines of distinction are often fluid. Therefore, it has rightly been characterised as being able to be put towards "both civilian and military uses, and more broadly, toward beneficial and harmful ends". It has also been said that, given that "some tasks that require intelligence are benign and other are not, artificial intelligence is dual-use in the same sense that human intelligence is".[158]

In terms of political security alone, several manipulative practices in the dual use of AI have been explicitly mentioned, including automated surveillance platforms to suppress dissent, fake news reports with realistic fabricated video and audio, automated and hyperpersonalised disinformation campaigns, denial-of-information attacks, and manipulation of information availability.[159] Another good example in this respect is provided by Google's (Alphabet Inc. corporation's) involvement in the Pentagon's "Project Maven", which is a program that "uses artificial intelligence to interpret video imagery, which could in turn be used to improve the targeting capability of drone strikes".[160]

For this reason, the proposed exemption of "AI systems developed or used exclusively for military purposes" in Article 2(3) AIA constitutes an important lacuna or "legal gap" in the proposed new legal framework. Moreover, it has been said to create a conflicting regulatory situation within the EU itself, formulated as follows:

> The exclusion of military AI from the scope of the Proposal is not only worrying given the risks associated with autonomous lethal weapons, it is also problematic considering that the European Union is itself actively involved in the development of military AI systems through the European Defence Fund. This involvement includes the development of the so-called "Eurodrone" which has the capacity to be armed. The Union itself could therefore be considered as actively contributing to the risks associated with autonomous lethal weapons.[161]

For this and other reasons, it is recommended that this gap in legal protection relating to military AI should be addressed and, ideally, all AI applications be brought within the future legal framework governing AI and eventually under the helm of the rule of law. Otherwise, the explicit permission for certain sectors or authorities to act beyond the law would constitute a form of institutional hypocrisy. Generally, a look at the existing technologies for AI and machine learning across various fields warrants the conclusion that it is extremely urgent and important to "develop more specific laws to govern an increasingly automated public sphere".[162] The prospects for future applications of AI, as well as the foreseeable convergence between military and civilian usages, only increase the urgency of the matter. Moreover, several existing and future AI systems and related technologies also invite more debates on the principles of new so-called "neurocrimes" and novel understandings of tort and causation for damages, including those caused by "cumulative harms". However, before any final conclusions are drawn, it will be useful to revisit other laws and cases which involve different kinds of subliminal techniques that are used with the intention of exerting various levels of mind control.

Notes

1 European Commission, *Proposal for a Regulation Laying Down Harmonised Rules on Artificial Intelligence (Artificial Intelligence Act)*, COM (2021) 206 final (21 April 2021) [AIA].

2 Regulation (EU) 2016/679 (General Data Protection Regulation), OJ L 119/1–88 (4 May 2016) [GDPR].
3 Adele Azzi, "The Challenges Faced by the Extraterritorial Scope of the General Data Protection Regulation" (2018) 9(2) *Journal of Intellectual Property, Information Technology and Electronic Commerce Law* 126–137.
4 Gráinne de Búrca, "Introduction to the Symposium on the GDPR and International Law" (2020) 114 *American Journal of International Law Unbound* 1–4, 1.
5 European Commission, *Proposal for a Regulation of the European Parliament and of the Council on contestable and fair markets in the digital sector (Digital Markets Act)*, COM(2020) 842 final (12 December 2020) [DMA].
6 European Commission, *Proposal for a Regulation of the European Parliament and of the Council on a Single Market For Digital Services (Digital Services Act) and amending Directive 2000/31/EC*, COM(2020) 825 final (15 December 2020) [DSA].
7 David Held, *Cosmopolitanism: Ideals and Realities* (Cambridge: Polity Press, 2010) 143.
8 Andrew Halpin and Volker Roeben (eds.), *Theorising the Global Legal Order* (Oxford: Hart, 2009) 6.
9 Michael Haenlein and Andreas Kaplan, "A Brief History of Artificial Intelligence: On the Past, Present, and Future of Artificial Intelligence" (2019) 61(4) *California Management Review* 5–14, 6–8 and Trevor Bench-Capon et al., "A history of AI and Law in 50 papers: 25 years of the international conference on AI and Law" (2012) 20 *Artificial Intelligence Law* 215–319, 215.
10 European Commission, *Artificial Intelligence for Europe*, COM(2018) 237 final (24 April 2018) 1.
11 *Ibid.*
12 *Ibid.*, 14 [footnote omitted].
13 *Ibid.*, 19.
14 European Commission, *Coordinated Plan on Artificial Intelligence*, COM (2018) 795 final (7 December 2018).
15 *Ibid.*, 6, 8–9.
16 High-Level Expert Group on AI (HLEG), *Ethics Guidelines for Trustworthy Artificial Intelligence* (8 April 2019); https://digital-strategy.ec.europa.eu/en/library/ethics-guidelines-trustworthy-ai.
17 European Commission, *Building Trust in Human-Centric Artificial Intelligence*, COM(2019) 168 final (8 April 2019).
18 *Ibid.*, 4–5.
19 *Ibid.*, 4–6.
20 High-Level Expert Group on AI, *Policy and Investment Recommendations for Trustworthy AI* (29 June 2019) 37; https://digital-strategy.ec.europa.eu/en/library/policy-and-investment-recommendations-trustworthy-artificial-intelligence.
21 European Commission, *Report on the safety and liability implications of Artificial Intelligence, the Internet of Things and robotics*, COM(2020) 64 final (19 February 2020) 3.
22 European Commission, *White Paper on Artificial Intelligence – A European approach to excellence and trust* COM(2020) 65 final (19 February 2020).

23 European Commission, *Fostering a European approach to Artificial Intelligence*, COM(2021) 205 final (21 April 2021) and European Commission, *Impact Assessment Accompanying the Proposal for a Regulation of the European Parliament and of the Council Laying Down Harmonised Rules on Artificial Intelligence (Artificial Intelligence Act) and Amending Certain Union Legislative* Acts, SWD(2021) 84 final (21 April 2021) [AI Impact Assessment].

24 GDPR (Regulation (EU) 2016/679), *supra* note 2; Directive (EU) 2016/680 (Law Enforcement Directive), OJ L 119/89–131 (4 May 2016). For a complete list of legislation seeking to harmonize EU legislation based on the proposed AIA, see Annex II ("List of Union Harmonisation Legislation") of the AIA, *supra* note 1.

25 Explanatory Memorandum of the AIA, *supra* note 1, 3.

26 Aviv H. Gaon, *The Future of Copyright in the Age of Artificial Intelligence* (Cheltenham: Edward Elgar, 2021) 51.

27 Ronald Chrisley "General Introduction: The Concept of Artificial Intelligence" in Ronald Chrisley and Sander Begeer (eds.) *Artificial Intelligence: Critical Concepts*, vol. 1 (New York: Routledge, 2000) 1–4, 3, Jennifer Gidley *The Future: A Very Short Introduction* (Oxford: Oxford University Press, 2017) 99 and Jakob Svensson, "Artificial intelligence is an oxymoron: The importance of an organic body when facing unknown situations as they unfold in the present moment" (2021) *AI & Society* 1–10, 8; https://doi.org/10.1007/s00146-021-01311-z.

28 Recital 6 and Art. 3(1) AIA, *supra* note 1.

29 European Commission, *Annexes to the Proposal for a Regulation of the European Parliament and of the Council Laying Down Harmonised Rules on Artificial Intelligence (Artificial Intelligence Act)*, COM(2021) 206 final (21 April 2021).

30 Art. 4 AIA, *supra* note 1.

31 Mark L. Johnson, "Mind, Metaphor, Law" (2007) 58(3) *Mercer Law Review* 845–860, 845.

32 Explanatory Memorandum of the AIA, *supra* note 1, 12.

33 *Ibid.*

34 Articles 8, 9 and 19 AIA, *supra* note 1.

35 Explanatory Memorandum and Article 52 AIA, *supra* note 1, 14.

36 Explanatory Memorandum of the AIA, *supra* note 1, 15.

37 Recital 72 and Art. 53 AIA, *supra* note 1.

38 Art. 69 AIA, *supra* note 1.

39 Art. 70 and 71 AIA, *supra* note 1.

40 Council of the European Union, *Presidency Compromise Text (AIA)*, 14278/21 (29 November 2021).

41 Andreas Kaplan, "Artificial Intelligence, Social Media, and Fake News: Is this the End of Democracy?" in Ayşen Akkor Gül, Yıldız Dilek Ertürk and Paul Elme (eds.), *Digital Transformation in Media & Society* (Istanbul: Istanbul University Press, 2020) 149–161, 150 and Susan Morgan, "Fake news, disinformation, manipulation and online tactics to undermine democracy" (2018) 3(1) *Journal of Cyber Policy* 39–43.

42 Ran R. Hassin et al., "Subliminal Exposure to National Flags Affects Political Thought and Behavior" (2007) 104(50) *Proceedings of the National Academy of Sciences (PNAS)* 19757–19761, 19760.

43 Robert Cialdini, *Pre-Suasion: A Revolutionary Way to Influence and Persuade* (New York: Simon & Schuster, 2016) 357, Alexander Todorov and John A. Bargh, "Automatic sources of aggression" (2002) 7 *Aggression and Violent Behavior* 53–68, 56 and Baptiste Subra et al., "Automatic Effects of Alcohol and Aggressive Cues on Aggressive Thoughts and Behaviors" (2010) 36(8) *Personality and Social Psychology Bulletin* 1052–1057, 1055.

44 G. Pascal Zachary, "Digital Manipulation and the Future of Electoral Democracy in the U.S." (2020) 1(2) *IEEE Transactions on Technology and Society* 104–112 and Terrell McSweeny, "Psychographics, Predictive Analytics, Artificial Intelligence, & Bots: is the FTC Keeping Pace?" (2018) 2 *Georgetown Law Technology Review* 514–530.

45 Bing Pan et al., "In Google we trust: User's decisions on rank, position, and relevance" (2007) 12(3) *Journal of Computer-Mediated Communication* 801–823, 801.

46 Robert Epstein and Ronald E. Robertson, "The search engine manipulation effect (SEME) and its possible impact on the outcomes of elections" (2015) 112(33) *Proceedings of the National Academy of Sciences (PNAS)* E4512-E4521, E4512.

47 Christian Djeffal, "AI, Democracy and the Law" in Andreas Sudmann (ed.), *The Democratization of Artificial Intelligence: Net Politics in the Era of Learning Algorithms* (Bielefeld: Transcript Verlag, 2019) 255–283, 279.

48 European Commission, *Study to Support an Impact Assessment of Regulatory Requirements for Artificial Intelligence in Europe: Final Report* (Luxembourg: Publications Office of the European Union, 2021) 31 [*Italics* added].

49 Luluah Albarrak, Oussama Metatla, and Anne Roudaut, "Exploring the influence of subliminal stimulus type and peripheral angle on the priming effect" (2021) 151 *International Journal of Human – Computer Studies* 1–17, 1.

50 Corina Cara, "Dark Patterns in the Media: A Systematic Review" (2019) 7(14) *Network Intelligence Studies* 105–113, 105.

51 Gregory Day and Abbey Stemler, "Are Dark Patterns Anticompetitive?" (2020) 72(1) *Alabama Law Review* 1–46, 2 and 45 [*Italics* added].

52 Ari Ezra Waldman, "Cognitive biases, dark patterns, and the 'privacy paradox'" (2020) 31 *Current Opinion in Psychology* 105–109, 105.

53 AI Impact Assessment, *supra* note 23, 17 [footnotes omitted; *Italics* added].

54 U.S. White House Office of Science and Technology Policy, *Request for Information on the Future of Artificial Intelligence* (1 September 2016) 31 [*Italics* added]; https://obamawhitehouse.archives.gov/sites/default/files/microsites/ostp/OSTP-AI-RFI-Responses.pdf.

55 AI Impact Assessment, *supra* note 23, 47.

56 Recital 16 AIA, *supra* note 1.

57 *Ibid.*

58 Art. 5(1) lit. a) AIA, *supra* note 1 [*Italics* added].

59 Ernest Klein, *A Comprehensive Etymological Dictionary of the English Language* (Amsterdam: Elsevier, 1966) 726.

60 A.J. Parker, "Sense and the Single Neuron: Probing the Physiology of Perception" (1998) 21 *Annual Review of Neuroscience* 227–277, 230.

61 G. Vithoulkas and D.F. Muresanu, "Conscience and Consciousness: A Definition" (2014) 7(1) *Journal of Medicine and Life* 104–108, 104.
62 Gunter Meissner, "Artificial intelligence: consciousness and conscience" (2020) 35 *AI & Society* 225–235, 232 [*Italics* added].
63 Vithoulkas and Muresanu, *supra* note 61, 104.
64 Gary R. VandenBos (ed.), *APA Dictionary of Psychology*, 2nd ed. (Washington: American Psychological Association, 2015) 1060.
65 David Matsumoto (ed.), *The Cambridge Dictionary of Psychology* (Cambridge: Cambridge University Press, 2009) 128.
66 Hillary S. Webb, "Dualism" in David A. Leeming (ed.), *Encyclopedia of Psychology and Religion*, 3rd ed. (Dordrecht: Springer, 2020) 702–705, 702 and Gabriel Segal, "Poverty of Stimulus Arguments Concerning Language and Folk Psychology" in Peter Carruthers, Stephen Laurence, and Stephen Stich (eds.), *The Innate Mind: Foundations and the Future*, vol. 3 (Oxford: Oxford University Press, 2008) 90–105, 101.
67 Matsumoto, *supra* note 65, 128, 525 and 559.
68 Ap Dijksterhuis, Henk Aarts, and Pamela K. Smith, "The Power of the Subliminal: On Subliminal Persuasion and Other Potential Applications" in Ran R. Hassin, James S. Uleman, and John A. Bargh (eds.), *The New Unconscious* (Oxford: Oxford University Press, 2005) 77–106, 99.
69 W. James Potter, *Media Literacy*, 8th ed. (Los Angeles: SAGE, 2016) 756–757.
70 Jonathan Miller, "The Mind's Eye and the Human Eye" (1985) 114(4) *Daedalus* 185–199.
71 Michael Pace, *Subliminal Psychology 101: How to Stealthily Penetrate, Influence, and Subdue Anyone's Mind without Them Suspecting a Thing* (Scotts Valley, CA: CreateSpace Publishing, 2018) 10–11.
72 David A. Statt (ed.), *The Concise Dictionary of Psychology*, 3rd ed. (London: Routledge, 2003) 129 [*Italics* added].
73 James Houran, Rense Lange and Dan Hooper, "Cross-Examining the Case for Precognition: Comment on Mossbridge and Radin (2018)" (2018) 5(1) *Psychology of Consciousness: Theory, Research, and Practice* 98–109, 102 and Bruce Greyson, "Comments on 'Does Paranormal Perception Occur in Near-Death Experiences?'" (2007) 25(4) *Journal of Near-Death Studies* 237–244.
74 Rocco J. Gennaro, *The Consciousness Paradox: Consciousness, Concepts, and Higher-Order Thoughts* (Cambridge, MA: The MIT Press, 2012) 2.
75 Michael A. Thalbourne and James Houran, "Transliminality, the Mental Experience Inventory, and tolerance of ambiguity" (2000) 28 *Personality and Individual Differences* 853–863, 853.
76 David T. Welsh and Lisa D. Ordóñez, "Conscience without Cognition: The Effects of Subconscious Priming on Ethical Behavior" (2014) 57(3) *The Academy of Management Journal* 723–742, 723.
77 Michael A. Thalbourne et al., "Transliminality, brain function, and synesthesia" (2001) 189(3) *Journal of Nervous and Mental Disease* 190–192 and Christine Simmonds-Moore, "Synesthesia and the Perception of Unseen Realities" (2020) 62(2) *Journal of Humanistic Psychology* 187–207, 187.
78 Simon Boag, "Making sense of subliminal perception" in Alexandra M. Columbus (ed.), *Advances in Psychology Research*, vol. 54 (New York: Nova Science, 2008) 117–139, 133.

79 Matsumoto, *supra* note 65, 527.
80 Della Thompson (ed.), *The Oxford Dictionary of Current English* (Oxford: Oxford University Press, 1993) 547.
81 Recital 1 of the Constitution of the World Health Organization, signed on 22 July 1946, 14 U.N.T.S. 186.
82 Betsy J. Grey, "Neuroscience, Emotional Harm, and Emotional Distress Tort Claims" (2007) 7(9) *The American Journal of Bioethics* 65–67 and Lily Tsoi et al., "Neural substrates for moral judgments of psychological versus physical harm" (2018) *Social Cognitive and Affective Neuroscience* 460–470.
83 UNESCO International Bioethics Committee (IBC), *Preliminary Draft Report of the IBC on Ethical Issues of Neurotechnology*, SHS/BIO/IBC-Ext/2021/3 (15 December 2020) 6.
84 Alex Garnett et al., "Neuroethics and fMRI: Mapping a Fledgling Relationship" (2011) 6(4) *PLoS ONE* 1–7, 1; doi:10.1371/journal.pone.0018537.
85 Mateja Durovic and Jonathon Watson, "Nothing to Be Happy about: Consumer Emotions and AI" (2021) 4(4) *J* 784–793, 792.
86 Jon A. Krosnick at al., "Subliminal Conditioning of Attitudes" (1992) 18(2) *Personality and Social Psychology* 152–162, 159 [In-text citations omitted].
87 Maha Nasrallah, David Carmel, and Nilli Lavie, "Murder, She Wrote: Enhanced Sensitivity to Negative Word Valence" (2009) 9(5) *Emotion* 609–618, 617.
88 Marc Trussler and Stuart Soroka, "Consumer Demand for Cynical and Negative News Frames" (2014) 19(3) *The International Journal of Press/Politics* 360–379, Richard Godfrey, "The politics of consuming war: video games, the military-entertainment complex and the spectacle of violence" (2021) *Journal of Marketing Management* 1–22; doi:10.1080/0267257X.2021.1995025, and Mochen Yang, Yuqing Ren, and Gediminas Adomavicius, "Understanding User-Generated Content and Customer Engagement on Facebook Business Pages" (2019) 30(3) *Information Systems Research* 839–855, 840.
89 Loren Coleman, *The Copycat Effect: How the Media and Popular Culture Trigger the Mayhem in Tomorrow's Headlines* (New York: Paraview Pocket Books, 2014) and Billy Crone, *Subliminal Seduction: How the Mass Media Mesmerize the Minds of the Masses* (Pahrump, NV: Get A Life Ministries Inc., 2021).
90 Nathalie Smuha et al., "How the EU Can Achieve Legally Trustworthy AI: A Response to the European Commission's Proposal for an Artificial Intelligence Act." (2021), 21; https://papers.ssrn.com/sol3/papers.cfm?abstract_id=3899991 [footnote omitted], Martin Ebers et al., "The European Commission's Proposal for an Artificial Intelligence Act—A Critical Assessment by Members of the Robotics and AI Law Society (RAILS)" 2021 4 *J* 589–603, 592; https://doi.org/10.3390/j4040043 [footnote omitted] and Risto Uuk, "Manipulation and the AI Act", The Future of Life Institute (18 January 2022); https://futureoflife.org/wp-content/uploads/2022/01/FLI-Manipulation_AI_Act.pdf?x49432.
91 Anthony M. Marino, "Monopoly, Liability and Regulation" (1988) 54 *Southern Economic Journal* 913–927, 913.

92 Michael Veale and Frederik Zuiderveen Borgesius, "Demystifying the Draft EU Artificial Intelligence Act" (2021) 22(4) *Computer Law Review International* 97–112, 102 [footnotes omitted].

93 ASA Ruling on Electrosensitivity-UK (Complaint Ref: A17–388045) (4 April 2018); https://www.asa.org.uk/rulings/electrosensitivity-uk-a17-388045.html.

94 *Ibid.*

95 European Commission, *Evaluation of Council Directive 85/374/EEC on the approximation of laws, regulations and administrative provisions of the Member States concerning liability for defective products* (Luxembourg: Publications Office of the European Union, 2018) 64–65.

96 Jane Pirkis and Merete Nordentoft, "Media Influences on Suicide and Attempted Suicide" in Rory C. O'Connor, Stephen Platt, and Jacki Gordon (eds.) *International Handbook of Suicide Prevention: Research, Policy and Practice* (Chichester: Wiley-Blackwell, 2011) 531–544, 540.

97 Jean M. Twenge et al., "Increases in Depressive Symptoms, Suicide-Related Outcomes, and Suicide Rates Among U.S. Adolescents After 2010 and Links to Increased New Media Screen Time" (2018) 6(1) *Clinical Psychological Science* 3–17, 15.

98 Rosemary Sedgwick et al., "Social media, internet use and suicide attempts in adolescents" (2019) 32(6) *Current Opinion in Psychiatry* 534–541, 540.

99 Vivienne Badaan et al., "Imagining better societies: A social psychological framework for the study of utopian thinking and collective action" (2020) 14(4) *Social and Personality Psychology Compass* 1–14.

100 Future of Life Institute (FLI), *FLI Position Paper on the EU AI Act* (August 2021) 4; https://futureoflife.org/wp-content/uploads/2021/08/FLI-Position-Paper-on-the-EU-AI-Act.pdf?x72900.

101 Miriam C. Buiten, "Towards Intelligent Regulation of Artificial Intelligence" (2019) 10 *European Journal of Risk Regulation* 41–59, 51.

102 Smuha et al., *supra* note 90, 21, Philipp Hacker, "Manipulation by Algorithms. Exploring the Triangle of Unfair Commercial Practice, Data Protection, and Privacy Law" (2021) *European Law Journal* 1–34, 28; https://doi.org/10.1111/eulj.12389.

103 María Triana, *Managing Diversity in Organizations: A Global Perspective* (New York: Routledge, 2017) 308.

104 Jonathan Heawood, "Pseudo-public political speech: Democratic implications of the Cambridge Analytica scandal" (2018) 23 *Information Polity* 429–434 and Tommaso Venturini and Richard Rogers, "'API-Based Research' or How can Digital Sociology and Journalism Studies Learn from the Facebook and Cambridge Analytica Data Breach" (2019) 7(4) *Digital Journalism* 532–540.

105 Council Directive 85/374/EEC (Product Liability Directive), OJ L 210/29 (7 August 1985) [PLD] and European Parliament, *Resolution of 20 October 2020 with recommendations to the Commission on a civil liability regime for artificial intelligence* (2020/2014(INL), P9_TA(2020)0276 (20 October 2020).

106 Jennifer G. Hill, "The Conundrum of Common Ownership" (2020) 53(3) *Vanderbilt Journal of Transnational Law* 881–906, 881.

107 Michael Duffy, "Climate Change Causation: Harmonizing Tort Law and Scientific Probability" (2019) 28(2) *Temple Journal of Science, Technology & Environmental Law* 185–242, 241.

108 Charles B. Kramer, "Judicial Recognition and Control of New Media Techniques: In Search of the Subliminal Tort" (1981) 14(3) *John Marshall Law Review* 733–760, 759.
109 Bernice B. Donald and Erica Bakies, "A Glimpse inside the Brain's Black Box: Understanding the Role of Neuroscience in Criminal Sentencing" (2016) 85(2) *Fordham Law Review* 481–502, 501–502.
110 Wiebe E. Bijker, Roland Bal and Ruud Hendriks, *Paradox of Scientific Authority: The Role of Scientific Advice in Democracies* (Cambridge, MA: MIT Press, 2009) 1 [footnote omitted].
111 European Commission, "Speech by Executive Vice-President Vestager at the press conference on fostering a European approach to Artificial Intelligence" (21 April 2021); https://ec.europa.eu/commission/presscorner/detail/en/SPEECH_21_1866.
112 Emmanuel Mogaji, Sunday Olaleye, and Dandison Ukpabi, "Using AI to Personalise Emotionally Appealing Advertisement" in Nripendra P. Rana et al. (eds.), *Digital and Social Media Marketing: Emerging Applications and Theoretical Development* (Cham: Springer, 2020) 137–150.
113 Silvia Klinčeková, "Neuromarketing – research and prediction of the future" (2016) 2(2) *International Journal of Management Science and Business Administration* 53–57, 53.
114 Letizia Alvino et al., "Picking Your Brains: Where and How Neuroscience Tools Can Enhance Marketing Research" (2020) 14 *Frontiers in Neuroscience* 1–25; doi:10.3389/fnins.2020.577666, Chiahui Yen and Ming-Chang Chiang, "Examining the effect of online advertisement cues on human responses using eye-tracking, EEG, and MRI" (2021) 402 (113128) *Behavioural Brain Research* 1–12; https://doi.org/10.1016/j.bbr.2021.113128 and Seyed Mojtaba Hosseini Bamakan, Aref Toghroljerdib, and Peyman Tirandazib, "Internet of Everything Driven Neuromarketing: Key Technologies and Challenges" (2021) *arXiv:2105.14470*; https://arxiv.org/abs/2105.14470.
115 Shekhar Suman et al., "Understanding and Improvisation of Human Perception Using Artificial Intelligence and Machine Learning" (2020) 1 (2) *Journal of Mathematical Sciences & Computational Mathematics* 251–256, 251.
116 Alexandros A. Lavdas, Nikos A. Salingaros, and Ann Sussman, "Visual Attention Software: A New Tool for Understanding the "Subliminal" Experience of the Built Environment" (2021) 11 *Applied Sciences* 1–29, 1 and 25; https://doi.org/10.3390/app11136197.
117 Jaap Ham, Cees Midden, and Femke Beute, "Can Ambient Persuasive Technology Persuade Unconsciously? Using Subliminal Feedback to Influence Energy Consumption Ratings of Household Appliances" (2009) 29 *Persuasive '09: Proceedings of the 4th International Conference on Persuasive Technology* 1–6, 4 and 5; https://doi.org/10.1145/1541948.1541988.
118 Blaise Pascal, *The Thoughts of Blaise Pascal* (London: Kegan Paul, Trench & Co., 1885) 57.
119 Robert Kraut et al., "Internet Paradox: A Social Technology that Reduces Social Involvement and Psychological Well-Being?" (1998) 53(9) *American Psychologist* 1017, 1029.
120 Rostam J. Neuwirth, *Law in the Time of Oxymora: A Synaesthesia of Language, Logic and Law* (New York: Routledge, 2018) 199.

121 Prem Melville and Vikas Sindhwani, "Recommender Systems" in Claude Sammut and Geoffrey I. Webb (eds.), *Encyclopedia of Machine Learning* (New York: Springer, 2011) 829–838, 829.

122 Mireille Hildebrandt, "The Issue of Proxies: And why EU law matters for recommender systems" (2021) *SocArXiv* 1–26, 3; doi:10.31235/osf.io/45x67.

123 Ira Steven Nathenson, "Internet Infoglut and Invisible Ink: Spamdexing Search Engines with Meta Tags" (1998) 12(1) *Harvard Journal of Law & Technology* 43–148, 46.

124 Nick Seaver, "Captivating algorithms: Recommender systems as traps" (2019) 24(4) *Journal of Material Culture* 421–436, 432.

125 Hildebrandt, *supra* note 122, 8–9.

126 Michael Dieter, "Dark Patterns: Interface Design, Augmentation and Crisis" in David M. Berry and Michael Dieter (eds.), *Postdigital Aesthetics: Art, Computation and Design* (Basingstoke: Palgrave Macmillan, 2015) 163–178, 174.

127 Liwei Hsu and Yen-Jung Chen, "Neuromarketing, subliminal advertising, and hotel selection: An EEG study" (2020) 28 *Australasian Marketing Journal* 200–208, 200.

128 Steven J. Stanton, Walter Sinnott-Armstrong, and Scott A. Huettel, "Neuromarketing: Ethical Implications of its Use and Potential Misuse" (2017) 144 *Journal of Business Ethics* 799–811.

129 Vinita Dawra Nangia "Are we being played by Artificial Intelligence?" *The Times of India* (10 October 2020); https://timesofindia.indiatimes.com/blogs/O-zone/are-we-being-played-by-artificial-intelligence/.

130 Frank Pasquale, *The Black Box Society: The Secret Algorithms that Control Money and Information* (Cambridge, MA: Harvard University Press, 2015) 4.

131 Timnit Gebru, "Data-Driven Claims about Race and Gender Perpetuate the Negative Biases of the Day" in Markus D. Dubber, Frank Pasquale and Sunit Das (eds.), *The Oxford Handbook of Ethics of AI* (Oxford: Oxford University Press, 2020) 253–269, 260.

132 Jean-Marc Rickli and Marcello Ienca, "The Security and Military Implications of Neurotechnology and Artificial Intelligence" in Orsolya Friedrich et al. (eds.), *Clinical Neurotechnology Meets Artificial Intelligence: Philosophical, Ethical, Legal and Social Implications* (Cham: Springer, 2021) 197–214, 207–208.

133 *Ibid.*, 197–214, 209.

134 Guillermo Bernal, Sean M. Montgomery and Pattie Maes, "Brain-Computer Interfaces, Open-Source, and Democratizing the Future of Augmented Consciousness" (2021) 3:661300 *Frontiers in Computer Science* 1–14, 10; https://doi.org/10.3389/fcomp.2021.661300.

135 Andreas Riener et al., "Subliminal Communication in Human-Computer Interaction" (2011) 2011 *Advances in Human-Computer Interaction* 1–3; https://doi.org/10.1155/2011/156028 and Walter Ritter, "Benefits of Subliminal Feedback Loops in Human-Computer Interaction" (2011) 2011 *Advances in Human-Computer Interaction* 1–11; https://doi.org/10.1155/2011/346492.

136 Vijay Chidambaram, Yueh-Hsuan Chiang and Bilge Mutlu, "Designing Persuasive Robots: How Robots Might Persuade People Using Vocal

and Nonverbal Cues" (2012) 2012 *7th ACM/IEEE International Conference on Human-Robot Interaction (HRI)* 293–300, 293; https://doi.org/10.1145/2157689.2157798.

137 Klaus Weber et al., "Towards Demystifying Subliminal Persuasiveness: Using XAI-Techniques to Highlight Persuasive Markers of Public Speeches" in Davide Calvaresi et al. (eds.), *Explainable, Transparent Autonomous Agents and Multi-Agent Systems* (Cham: Springer, 2020) 113–128.

138 Rostam J. Neuwirth, "The Regulation of 'Fake News' in the Time of Oxymora: Facts and Fictions about the Covid-19 Pandemic as Coincidences or Predictive Programming?" (2021) *International Journal for the Semiotics of Law* 1–27; https://doi.org/10.1007/s11196-021-09840-y.

139 Ivan Martinovic et al., "On the feasibility of side-channel attacks with brain-computer interfaces" (2012) *Proceedings of the 21st USENIX Security Symposium*, 143–158, 145; https://www.usenix.org/conference/usenixsecurity12/technical-sessions/presentation/martinovic.

140 Dustin Steinhagen and Houssain Kettani, "An Inventory of Existing Neuroprivacy Controls" (2020) *ICISDM 2020: Proceedings of the 2020 the 4th International Conference on Information System and Data Mining* 77–83, 78; https://doi.org/10.1145/3404663.3404664.

141 Mario Frank et al. "Using EEG-based BCI devices to subliminally probe for private information" (2017) *Proceedings of the 2017 Workshop on Privacy in the Electronic Society (WPES'17)* 133–136, 133; https://doi.org/10.1145/3139550.3139559.

142 Judith Amores and Pattie Maes, "Influencing Human Behavior by Means of Subliminal Stimuli using Scent, Light and Brain Computer Interfaces" (2016) *PETRA '16: Proceedings of the 9th ACM International Conference on PErvasive Technologies Related to Assistive Environments* 1–4; https://doi.org/10.1145/2910674.2935853.

143 J.F. Pagel, "Non-dreamers" (2003) 4(3) *Sleep Medicine* 235–241, 235.

144 Adam Haar Horowitz et al., "Dormio: A Targeted Dream Incubation Device" (2020) 83 *Consciousness and Cognition* 1–28, 2; https://doi.org/10.1016/j.concog.2020.102938.

145 Tore Nielsen, *Dream incubation: ancient techniques of dream influence* (Montreal: Dream & Nightmare Laboratory, 2012); http://www.dreamscience.ca/en/documents/New%20content/incubation/Incubation%20overview%20for%20website%20updated.pdf.

146 Adam Haar Horowitz, Robert Stickgold, and Antonio Zadra, "Inside your dreamscape", *Aeon* (19 November 2021); https://aeon.co/essays/dreams-are-a-precious-resource-dont-let-advertisers-hack-them.

147 Sizhi Ai et al., "Promoting subjective preferences in simple economic choices during nap" (2018) 7(e40583) *eLife* 1–21, 1; https://doi.org/10.7554/eLife.40583.

148 Charles Fisher and I.H. Paul, "The effect of subliminal visual stimulation on images and dreams: A validation study" (1959) 7 *Journal of the American Psychoanalytic Association* 35–83, 80.

149 Michael Prost, "Unconsciousness, Subconsciousness & the Creation of Consciousness" (2019) 10(5) *Journal of Consciousness Exploration & Research* 380–390 383.

150 Bernd W. Wirtz, Jan C. Weyerer, and Benjamin J. Sturm, "The Dark Sides of Artificial Intelligence: An Integrated AI Governance

Framework for Public Administration" (2020) 43(9) *International Journal of Public Administration* 818–829, 820–822.

151 Qiongfeng Shi et al., "Progress in wearable electronics/photonics—Moving toward the era of artificial intelligence and internet of things" (2020) 2 *InfoMat* 1131–1162; https://doi.org/10.1002/inf2.12122.

152 Tara J. Brigham, "Merging Technology and Emotions: Introduction to Affective Computing" (2017) 36(4) *Medical Reference Services Quarterly* 399–407, 405.

153 Giovanni Briganti and Olivier Le Moine, "Artificial Intelligence in Medicine: Today and Tomorrow" (2021) 7(27) *Frontiers in Medicine* 1–6, 4; https://doi.org/10.3389/fmed.2020.00027.

154 Evonne Miller and Debra Polson, "Apps, Avatars, and Robots: The Future of Mental Healthcare" (2019) 40(3) *Issues in Mental Health Nursing* 208–214, 208; https://doi.org/10.1080/01612840.2018.1524535.

155 Niklas Masuhr, "AI in Military Enabling Applications" *CSSCSS Analyses in Security Policy* (Center for Security Studies (CSS), ETH Zurich (29 October 2019); https://doi.org/10.3929/ethz-b-000367663.

156 Simon Chesterman, "Artificial Intelligence and the Problem of Autonomy" (2020) 1(2) *Notre Dame Journal on Emerging Technologies* 210–250, 248.

157 Roger Clarke, "Why the world wants controls over Artificial Intelligence" (2019) 35 *Computer Law & Security Review* 423–433, 427.

158 Miles Brundage et al., "The Malicious Use of Artificial Intelligence: Forecasting, Prevention, and Mitigation" Future of Humanity Institute, University of Oxford (February 2018) 16; https://arxiv.org/ftp/arxiv/papers/1802/1802.07228.pdf.

159 *Ibid.*, 28–29.

160 Penny Crofts and Honni van Rijswijk, "Negotiating 'Evil': Google, Project Maven and the Corporate Form" (2020) 2(1) *Law, Technology and Humans* 1–16, 1; https://doi.org/10.5204/lthj.v2i1.1313.

161 Smuha et al., *supra* note 90, 18 [footnote omitted].

162 Frank Pasquale, *New Laws of Robotics: Defending Human Expertise in the Age of AI* (Cambridge, MA: The Belknap Press, 2020) 110.

2 Subliminal perception and the law

Before looking at the connection between subliminal perception and the law, it is important to mention that according to the latest scientific findings and a new understanding of the unconscious, only 5% of our entire cognitive functions are conscious, while the remaining 95% are beyond our awareness but still exert an important influence on our lives.[1] In order to make the best assessment of the adequacy of the proposed prohibition of AI systems that deploy subliminal techniques, it is first useful to search for past regulatory approaches to the problem of subliminal perception. In this regard, the foremost example is provided by the prohibition of the practice of subliminal advertising that has been adopted by the EU as well as several other jurisdictions around the world. Before a closer look is taken at these laws, it is useful to look at the issue of subliminal advertising alone.

A Motivational research and "hidden persuaders"

The interest in subliminal or unnoticed sources of information goes back to the early dawn of humanity. The Ancient Greek philosopher Democritus is said to have believed that "much is perceptible which is not perceived by us, because it is not adapted to our senses".[2] In modern times, the Viennese neurologist Otto Pötzl is credited with having made, in the early twentieth century, one of the first scientifically significant discoveries about subliminal perception.[3] His findings were termed the "Pötzl phenomenon", which holds that "words or images that are presented subliminally may appear in imagery or dreams a short time later".[4] This phenomenon indicates an interesting link between conscious, subconscious or sleeping states of mind. Soon thereafter, attempts were made to apply these psychological findings to the field of market research.[5] Hence, it was motivational research that built the bridge between psychology and the applied science of marketing.[6]

DOI: 10.4324/9781003319436-3

Nowadays, the phenomenon of subliminal advertising is most commonly associated with an experiment using a tachistoscope (a machine that flashes on a screen invisible messages that can be seen by the subconscious) for 1/3000 of a second every five seconds to project subliminal messages, written in white letters and reading "Eat Popcorn" and "Drink Coca-Cola", during the screening of a film in a movie theatre in the US in 1957.[7] The said experiment was reported to have considerably boosted the sales for popcorn (by 57.1%) and Coca-Cola (by 18.1%). The origin of this association goes back to James Vicary, who was interested in applying psychology to market research.[8] The possible impact of subliminal advertising on behaviour received wider attention following the publication by Vance Packard of the book *The Hidden Persuaders.*[9] In his conclusion, the author wrote:

> The most serious offense many of the depth manipulators commit, it seems to me, is that they try to invade the privacy of our minds. It is this right to privacy in our minds—privacy to be either rational or irrational—that I believe we must strive to protect.[10]

Not long ago, the debate about the effectiveness of subliminal advertising was still overshadowed by the controversy about the findings presented by James Vicary, as his experiments were often said to have been a hoax and were thus called a myth.[11] Perhaps it was because of the possible hoax that the question about the effect of subliminal stimuli was not taken seriously, and remained contested for quite some time. For instance, in the late 1990s it was reported that leading journals remained divided on the issue of subliminal advertising.[12] This is also the main reason why it is still often falsely assumed that subliminal advertising does not work.[13]

Today, however, the general effect of subliminal stimuli can be taken as scientifically proven. In 2006, two similar experiments were carried out, which aimed to assess "whether subliminal priming of a brand name of a drink can affect people's choices for the primed brand, and whether this effect is moderated by individuals' feelings of thirst".[14] The findings in both studies confirmed that "subliminal priming of a brand name of drink (i.e., Lipton Ice) positively affected participants' choice for, and their intention to, drink the primed brand, but only for participants who were thirsty".[15] At roughly the same time, the past controversy was revisited, leading to the conclusion that "where there remains some controversy over the extent or nature of the behavior that can be influenced by subliminal messages, there is little doubt that properly presented subliminal information is processed, retained, and *acted upon*".[16] Here, clearly, the crucial point is the finding that – as in the case of metaphors – subliminal messages not only affect human thoughts but actually alter human actions as well.[17] Lastly, in 2011 an editorial note stated that in the field of neuromarketing the effectiveness of subliminal priming is no longer a question of *whether*, but rather of *how*, it influences consumer behaviour.[18]

More research has confirmed that there are multiple forms of subliminal persuasion. For instance, priming can be triggered when the "presentation of a word or sign influences the way in which participants interpret a subsequent word or sign", and it is then called "semantic priming".[19] In this context too, one of the most controversial questions is about the dichotomy of "conscious versus unconscious" or "subliminal versus supraliminal" brain perception.[20] Put briefly, this question asks whether semantic priming can "occur even when the prime is presented under conditions in which it cannot be identified or its presence cannot be detected".[21] Generally, priming seems to confirm that subliminal and supraliminal techniques are effective but depend to a large degree on various additional factors, such as the frequency of the exposure,[22] and characteristics related to personality,[23] like interest, motivation, awareness or the prevalence of a particular precondition in the consumer or target.[24] In this situation, in particular, the combination of the collection of big data, profiling, targeted advertisements, and other "immersive" and neuromarketing-based applications can be expected to enhance the overall efficiency of subliminal stimuli.[25] This is already the case with personalised forms of advertisement, which has been outlined as follows:

> Personalized advertisement is in fact trying to manipulate people's choices, based on the detailed knowledge of a person, including how he/she thinks, feels, and responds to certain kinds of situations. These approaches become increasingly effective, making use of biases in human decision-making and also *subliminal messages*. Such techniques address people's subconsciousness, such that they would not necessarily be aware of the reasons causing their actions, similar to acting under hypnosis.[26]

The various persuasive technologies have also been defined as "any interactive computing system designed to change people's attitudes or behaviors".[27] The use of subliminal techniques in advertisement is certainly set to increase. Akin to or synonymous with the notions of "dark patterns", "subliminal persuasion" or "subliminal priming", these techniques are not restricted to advertisement and marketing. On the contrary, the same subliminal techniques are already and will increasingly be applied to other areas, such as public relations, propaganda, negotiation, and even religion, to mention but a few.[28]

Even in the fields of law and policy-making, analogies have been drawn between subliminal advertisements and manipulative practices known as "nudging" that are followed in order to further certain policy goals.[29] Nudging, also termed "a modern form of paternalism", will also be greatly helped by the use of big data and AI, and warnings have already been given that nudges in combination with misinformation and power abuse and in the shadow of subliminal manipulation can prove detrimental to people's democratic rights.[30] At the same time, nudging has also been commended as a way to address the potential dangers inherent in the lack of regulation for AI, as "advances in regulatory capacity have not kept pace with developments in new technologies, including AI".[31] Overall, the trend in nudging and artificial intelligence has been said to show a move from "*programming computers to programming people*".[32]

In advertisement in general, three different forms of manipulation can be distinguished, namely subliminal, disguised, and distorting advertisements, but the essential characteristic of all three is the principle of concealment, which means that the targeted person is not conscious of being manipulated but instead believes that she/he can make a decision free from influence.[33] Concealment is also one of the invisible forms of manipulation in the context of the manipulation of political views.[34] Conversely, subliminal forms of manipulation must be regarded as the most sophisticated forms of concealment.

This marks an important observation against the backdrop of a constant trend of the convergence of technologies and industries, not limited to the media, biotechnology, and nanotechnology.[35] Subliminal techniques must be monitored across various sectors and by using transdisciplinary and comprehensive approaches, if regulation is to make a difference in life and in reality. It is now scientifically sound to state that subliminal messages have an effect on the mind. Moreover, it has been found that AI techniques deploying subliminal techniques will increase both in quality and in quantity in the near future. This is why priming research has been found to be relevant, not only for marketing but also for a wider area of sciences, including, but not limited to, public health and politics.[36] The potentially transformative impact of AI, and progress in breaking the barriers to the individual mind, raise important questions about the role of law, not only in regulating AI but also in controlling people's behaviour in the future.

With regard to this last point, it is therefore interesting to look at past regulatory efforts targeting subliminal forms of persuasion.

B Laws prohibiting subliminal advertising

The fact that many jurisdictions around the world adopted laws and regulations prohibiting various subliminal forms of commercial advertising more than three decades ago is a strong indicator of the effectiveness of mind control at large. In Europe, the Council of Europe prepared the European Convention on Transfrontier Television (ECTT), which was adopted in May 1989, and this contains a provision stipulating that "advertising and tele-shopping shall not use subliminal techniques".[37] There is little information today about the motives that originally triggered the decision to include this prohibition in the text of the Convention. It seems that the concerns can be traced back to the book *The Hidden Persuaders* and to examples about subliminal ice cream, Coca-Cola, and popcorn advertisements, notwithstanding that their effectiveness was considered controversial at the time.[38]

A few months later, the EU's predecessor, the European Economic Community, adopted a similar law by virtue of the 1989 Television Without Frontiers Directive (TWFD), which contained a similar prohibition.[39] The text of the TWFD's prohibition of subliminal advertising was amended in order achieve greater coherence with the text of the ECTT.[40] This Directive formed the basis of the current European law regulating this matter, the EU's Audiovisual Media Services Directive (AVMSD), which stipulates as follows:

> Article 9 AVMSD
>
> 1. Member States shall ensure that audiovisual commercial communications provided by media service providers under their jurisdiction comply with the following requirements:
>
> (a) audiovisual commercial communications shall be readily recognisable as such; surreptitious audiovisual commercial communication shall be prohibited;
>
> (b) *audiovisual commercial communications shall not use subliminal techniques.*[41]

The widespread prohibition of audiovisual commercial communications that use subliminal techniques may provide a useful precedent for the proposed prohibition of AI systems deploying these same techniques. Among the reasons is, first, the fact that the earlier scientific controversy about the effectiveness of subliminal advertising is now generally settled in favour of the claim that it has effects on the targeted users or consumers. Second, the technologies used for subliminal techniques have not only improved drastically since the late 1980s, but can be expected to improve rapidly again in the near future, especially on the basis of advances in neuroscience and related technologies (e.g. BCIs), which will also gradually lead to a greater integration of the individual senses.

Therefore, the key question about the future effectiveness of the relevant provision in the AIA will be how it functions as a deterrent for the abusive and harmful use of AI systems that deploy subliminal techniques. This requires us to think in advance of the entry into force of Art. 5(1) AIA, to prepare for the best possible enforcement mechanisms to be put in place. To improve the enforcement of the AIA, it is therefore important to take stock and inspiration from the relevant provisions in the AVMSD that are currently in force, and the experiences gained from the enforcement of this Directive. Unfortunately, despite the prohibition of subliminal advertising having been in force in Europe for more than three decades, evidence from relevant case law is very thin. Moreover, it seems that the competent regulatory and supervisory bodies have little interest in monitoring the prohibition of subliminal advertising.

The fact is that there exists a plethora of regulatory bodies that oversee the implementation of and compliance with the said laws and regulations. These include the Council of Europe,[42] the European Broadcasting Union (EBU),[43] the European Platform of Regulatory Authorities (EPRA),[44] the European Advertising Standards Alliance (EASA),[45] and the European Regulators Group for Audiovisual Media Services (ERGA).[46] The work of these international or supranational regulatory bodies is supplemented by numerous national regulatory bodies, such as Ofcom in the UK, the Conseil Supérieur de l'Audiovisuel (CSA) in France, the Direktorenkonferenz der Landesmedienanstalten in Germany, the Autorità per le Garanzie nelle Comunicazioni (AGCOM) in Italy, and Kommunikationsbehörde Austria (KommAustria).[47]

However, various searches on their websites as well as email contact with these agencies suggest that there are no particular cases on record regarding subliminal advertising. This is likely to be due to a lack of monitoring in this area, which, however, should not lead to the conclusion that the problem does not exist even just in advertising.[48] Additionally, several national authorities did not reply to the relevant emails sent. Ofcom replied, but suggested that the UK's Advertising

Standards Authority (ASA) should be contacted instead, and unfortunately no reply was received from the ASA. A reply received from KommAustria, the Austrian regulatory authority, contained information about a past case that allegedly involved a subliminal advertisement for dog food. To promote the product, this ad was suspected of having used tones imperceptible to humans but not to dogs, as dogs seemed to have reacted to it. Since the addressees of the prohibited activity must be humans and not animals, the case was not investigated further.[49]

Other enquiries concerned the actual means for the enforcement of the provisions through the monitoring of the content of broadcasts. In this regard, there is also little to report, as the regulators do not seem to monitor the content constantly but merely to carry out random checks from time to time. As a new challenge, there are also serious concerns raised by various regulators about disguised advertising formats that are not recognisable, such as photos and videos posted on social media, or other materials used by "web influencers" and vloggers and in so-called "celebrity endorsements". In this respect, concerns have been raised about the adequacy of existing laws, and especially about whether a model of self-regulation and voluntary commitments will be enough on its own.[50] In sum, there seems to be a significant imbalance in the efforts to regulate subliminal advertisements, on the one hand, and the efforts to enforce the relevant provisions, on the other. This should be read as a warning for the AIA, which is why, before it enters into force, the necessary arrangements must be made to ensure the effective monitoring of any subliminal techniques that are deployed, and the enforcement of the prohibition.

Overall, this situation also raises serious concerns about the future efficacy of the planned prohibition for AI systems, because it is not clear whether, how, and by whom the relevant provision would be enforced in order to secure compliance. It is most likely that the enforcement would require a comprehensive monitoring effort, paradoxically using AI systems that have been developed to detect AI systems using subliminal techniques. Additionally, it will be necessary to have fewer, but more efficient, regulatory authorities monitoring the use of AI systems deploying subliminal techniques and ensuring enforcement, as otherwise the relevant provisions in the AIA will be "dead letter law".

Given the uncertainty about the effectiveness of prohibitions on subliminal advertising in Europe, as well as the expected extraterritorial effects of the planned regulation, it will also be beneficial to take a brief look beyond the regulatory boundaries of Europe. Similar prohibitions can be found elsewhere, such as in Russia,[51] the People's Republic of China,[52] and China's Macao Special Administrative Region.[53] India too has relevant rules, but no uniform code of law on advertising. Instead, it relies on self-regulatory approaches set by the Advertising Standards Council of India (ASCI), which has adopted a Code for Self-Regulation in Advertising that also aims "to safeguard against misleading advertisements" but does not explicitly specify subliminal advertisements.[54] It is noteworthy that the ASCI has recently adopted Guidelines for Social Influencers, which require that disclosure statements are made clearly visible (e.g. "for videos that last 15 seconds or less, the disclosure label must stay for a minimum of 3 seconds") so that the average consumer is able to see them clearly.[55] Generally, there seems to be a global consensus that "marketing communications should be truthful and not misleading".[56] Given the proliferation of subliminal videos on social media and video platforms, there is also a major case for a global prohibition of new media and AI systems deploying subliminal techniques.

As far as the United States is concerned, the situation is complex, and quite contradictory statements about past and current regulation can be found in the relevant legal literature. The US has a long history on the issue of subliminal advertising, as the 1957 case of James Vicary and the book *The Hidden Persuaders* originated in the US market.[57] However, it has been said that although there was "an uproar over subliminal advertising, the legal response to neuromarketing has been muted at best".[58] In 2021 it was reported that representatives had introduced bills in 1958 to make the use of subliminal advertising on television unlawful, but that no hearings were ever organised, and there is no law on subliminal messages.[59]

Nevertheless, there are general provisions of relevance to the issue. The federal statute that in 1914 established the Federal Trade Commission (FTC), which is the regulatory authority in charge of protecting consumers by stopping unfair, deceptive or fraudulent practices in the marketplace, also contains provisions to prevent the dissemination of false advertisements, which is deemed "an unfair or deceptive act or practice in or affecting commerce".[60] The definition of "false advertisement" reads as follows:

> (1) The term "false advertisement" means an advertisement, other than labeling, which is misleading in a material respect; and in determining whether any advertisement is misleading, there shall be taken into account (among other things) not only representations made or suggested by statement, word, design, device,

> sound, or any combination thereof, but also the extent to which the advertisement fails to reveal facts material in the light of such representations or material with respect to consequences which may result from the use of the commodity to which the advertisement relates under the conditions prescribed in said advertisement, or under such conditions as are customary or usual.[61]

Given that the definition also uses the term "misleading" for false advertisements and that the criteria to be taken into account are merely illustrative and not exhaustive, it is possible to conclude that subliminal messages in advertisements can also fall within the scope of this prohibition.

Complicating the issue in the US system is that there is no uniform advertisement law. Instead, several special laws have been adopted for advertisements in specific sectors, such as tobacco, alcohol, firearms, cosmetics, and food. Even in the early years, it was suggested that "much of TV advertising's persuasive impact is not consciously perceived at all and is in fact a type of subliminal influence on consumer decision-making, an influence deserving of closer attention and regulation by the Federal Trade Commission".[62] With regard to the controversy surrounding the effectiveness of subliminal advertisements, it was also stated that the "use of such techniques may not at first seem effective at selling a product; however, they are successful in affecting the viewer and facilitating a purchase", and the conclusion was reached that "it is time that the law recognize the coercive power of subliminal messages in tobacco advertising, and enact the foregoing proposed prohibition on the use of subliminals by the tobacco industry".[63]

Recently, the claim was repeated that there currently exists no specific federal law in the US that explicitly prohibits subliminal messages or forms of neuromarketing.[64] Today, relevant information on the FTC website merely contains one reference to subliminal advertising in its Q&A section, as follows:

> Is it legal to use subliminal advertising techniques?
> It would be deceptive for marketers to embed ads with so-called subliminal messages that could affect consumer behavior. However, most consumer behavior experts have concluded that such methods aren't effective.[65]

This suggests that subliminal advertisements are outlawed, even though they are not considered to be effective, which, however, stands in stark contrast to the scientific findings and experiments described above. It also contradicts the information provided by the FTC, that "under the law, claims in advertisements must be truthful, cannot be deceptive or unfair, and must be evidence-based".[66] In this regard, more recent scientific evidence seems to suggest that various subliminal forms are already effective and will become even more so in the future.

For the regulation of subliminal techniques in the future, however, the past academic debates in the US provide a rich and fertile ground. As early as 1981, a comprehensive analysis of what was then called "Subliminal Communication Technology" was published as an article. Reading the introduction, it is interesting to note the parallels to the debate today:

> Debates about the moral, legal, and ethical dilemmas posed by various forms of behavior control are not a recent development. However, current technological innovations in this area have generated heated debate over newly created problems that are not easily resolved by reference to any traditional framework for evaluating issues and solutions.[67]

This suggests that, back then, the issue of subliminal techniques deployed by different means also caused concern for the consistency of the legal system as a whole and the specific relationship between different laws and regulations.

In spite of the absence of an explicit prohibition of subliminal advertising, the US legal system has contributed numerous important elements to the issue of subliminal persuasion, and these are useful for gaining an understanding of subliminal perception in the context of new technologies, and AI systems deploying subliminal persuasion techniques. For instance, the topic was addressed in the field of trademark law under the term "subliminal confusion" or "subliminal trademark association". This type of confusion was recognised by several courts as actionable under the trademark law as a way to remedy what was called "an elusive, cognitive consumer injury".[68] Unlike subliminal advertising, subliminal trademark confusion does not mislead the consumer of a product but still affects "a buyer's perception of a product through an unconscious or subliminal association of marks".[69]

Other important aspects derive from several cases concerned with subliminal messages transmitted through both visual and auditory means. In addition to Vicary's visual popcorn experiment, there are also reports about a kind of "electronic conscience" used in order to prevent shoplifting, in the form of subliminal messages encoded in the background music playing throughout a store.[70]

Even in an article published in 1982, it was found that subliminal persuasion is ubiquitous and that the "mechanics of subliminal persuasion follow advances in media technology".[71] It should be noted that these advances in technology mean that people are being subjected to subliminal messages during many of their daily activities, through television, movies, magazines and even department stores that "expose the public to messages below the threshold of conscious perception".[72] A wider consideration of subliminal forms of persuasion has also prompted questions about their potential conflict with free speech as guaranteed by the First Amendment.[73] In particular, this concerns the question of whether subliminal messages fall within the notion of language or speech, as subliminals generally remain unconscious and do not surface in normal conversation.[74]

The problem of subliminal messages remaining hidden is also found in the form of backward masking, which refers to the embedding of reversed speech in music.[75] Generally, in perception, masking refers to "the partial or complete obscuring of one stimulus (the target) by another (the masker)".[76] It is important to add that these stimuli can be used for all senses, meaning they can be visual images, sounds, tastes, odorants or even tactile stimuli. Moreover, the masker can be presented before ("forward masking"), after ("backward masking") or at the same time as ("simultaneous masking") the target stimulus.[77] This technique has been related to several suicides in the US, which were allegedly caused by subliminal messages in the form of masked or subliminal lyrics embedded in rock and heavy metal music. The most cited lawsuits were those against the rock band Judas Priest and the heavy metal musician Ozzy Osbourne, who were accused of inciting four teenagers to commit and a fifth to attempt suicide.[78] It is interesting to note that the courts examined not only the history of subliminal communication technology but also the CIA's apparent interest in using subliminal messages to influence the results of political elections.[79] Obscured by the misleading labels of "hoax" or "conspiracy theory", it is still difficult today to find reliable information about the CIA's activities in experiments involving subliminals and mind control, like those associated with MKUltra, even though it was later established that MKUltra did exist.[80]

The case against Judas Priest, in particular, was widely publicised and commented upon in the literature.[81] In the end the lawsuit did not hold Judas Priest liable for the deaths of the teenagers even though some subliminal messages were found in the music concerned, because of "the insufficiency of the plaintiffs' evidence in proving the element of 'intent'".[82] These precedents from three decades ago may become more relevant again in the context of AI-generated music. Music has not only been called one of the most esteemed forms of art but it also "conveys ideas as well as emotions at the subliminal level".[83] Having background music played in shops has been shown to lead to higher sales.[84] Thus, if AI using algorithms can already automate the composition of music, it will also be possible to enhance the modes by which subliminal messages can be added to this art form, which already operates to a large extent at all levels of consciousness. Already, there exist studies showing that music has an impact on the listener and "does correlate with anti-social outcomes".[85] These studies confirm earlier findings on the effects of the exposure to subliminal stimuli.[86] These effects were found to be greater in the case when the exposure was repeated. In this regard, a finding that is also important for the present prohibition of subliminal techniques is that not only are subliminal stimuli more intrusive when they are flashed frequently but also that "exposure effects are more pronounced when obtained under subliminal conditions than when subjects are aware of the repeated exposures".[87] This marks a strong argument for a prohibition of subliminal techniques and not merely a requirement to make them evident for the sake of transparency.

However, to cut a long story short, these cases show the complexity of the problem of subliminal persuasion as a whole, in both scientific and legal terms. From a scientific perspective, subliminal persuasion reflects a limited understanding of the brain, of cognition and of language, as well as a focus on physical constituents, which – hampered by a lack of unity in science – translate into the lack of a general scientific consensus across different disciplines on the matter.[88] From a legal perspective, the problems are similar. In law, the various forms or techniques of subliminal persuasion clash with the law's general tendency to neglect, or its reluctance to accept, the existence of intangible, emotional or other non-material concerns, all of which are aggravated by the current fragmentation of laws and an excessive focus on ocularcentrism, that is, "the epistemological prioritization of sight above other human senses".[89] For the future of law, this means joining forces with science and seeking a better coordination of the mutual relationship between different laws, such as those governing freedom of expression and freedom of thought, as well as laws on AI, privacy, product liability, advertisements, trademarks, and torts, to mention but a few. In view of the frequent tendency to overregulation and legislative zeal, less regulation can, paradoxically, mean more, not only in terms of the expected outcomes but also in terms of regulatory certainty and predictability as a whole.

C Subliminal perception and the senses: between individuality and unity

Further complicating the issue of subliminal persuasion is that it involves not only the transmitter of such messages but also the receiver, mostly through the human sensory apparatus. In other words, AI will drastically alter the means for transmitting content and information subliminally but will not affect one sensory channel alone. It can be expected that the different devices and applications being developed will be able to stimulate one, two or more senses, as well as all the senses simultaneously. This also requires us to take a closer look at the side of the receiver and at AI's impact on the senses, both individually and taken together.

So far, most of the examples given of subliminal messages have been either of a visual or of an auditory nature. Only occasionally have other senses, such as olfaction, taste, and touch, which are equally susceptible to subliminal sensations, been mentioned. This is important because before the mind is exposed to subliminal techniques, the message is captured by the senses. Thus, to determine whether a message is "subliminal", that is, below the threshold of awareness, a different assessment is required for each individual sense. One particular problem in this respect is that historically the number of senses has been fixed at five, namely seeing, hearing, touching, tasting, and smelling.[90] An additional problem is that each of these five senses has traditionally been studied in isolation.[91] As a result, we seem to know the exact information transmission rates of each of the senses, which range from 10,000,000 bits per second for the eyes to only 1,000 for taste.[92] This may also explain why vision is usually ranked first, and also why law has earned the criticism of being too "ocularcentric".[93] Both the limitation to only five senses and the study of each sense in isolation appear problematic and have been critically questioned as follows:

> We often think about our senses as separate and independent of each other. However, there are at least four problems with this *naïve view.* First, our experience of the world around us is a rich multisensory one. Under normal conditions, our senses are constantly flooded with information. [...] Second, our sensations do

> seem to come together somehow into a unified experience. The sights and sounds of most events we witness do not appear to be two independent streams of information; in fact, they seem inseparable. A third problem is that the senses do not merely converge somewhere; they also influence each other. [...] The fourth reason to doubt the independence of the senses is that, for some individuals, stimulation in one sensory modality may actually give rise to perceptual experience in more than one modality.[94]

In other words, although the senses differ individually, they also mutually influence each other and potentially give rise to an integrated or multisensory experience that is more than the mere sum of the experience of the individual senses. Such a multisensory experience of reality is also captured by synaesthesia, which explains why it is vital to look more closely at the different ways in which individual senses interact with and also affect each other.

To begin with vision, the interaction between seeing and hearing probably occurs more often, given the prevalence of audiovisual media. An example of their interaction is found in speech perception, which – contrary to the first impression – is not an exclusively auditory process. In a study published with the title *Hearing Lips and Seeing Voices*, it was shown that even speech perception involves visual elements in the form of lip movements; this came to be known as the McGurk effect.[95] Obviously, facial expressions, gesticulations and body language as a whole also provide visual clues as to the meaning of what is heard. Body language has even been referred to as "visible thoughts".[96] This is also an important reminder of the potential consequences of facial recognition technology for speech recognition. Technology already exists that allows one to read lips from silent video or film recordings, by decoding text from the movement of the speaker's mouth.[97] The potential of such technology was shown, for instance, in the possibility of successfully deciphering, from his lip movements alone, the words spoken by Adolf Hitler in a private silent movie recording.[98] Surprisingly, the same technology even works for tone-based languages like Chinese Mandarin. This is indeed surprising because tonal languages evidently significantly increase the ambiguity in the lip reading task.[99] For a long time, the emergence of new biometric technologies, in combination with other technologies such as video surveillance, has given rise to concerns and calls for a general right to privacy or the extension of privacy rights to public areas.[100] In short, it shows that, seemingly paradoxically, communication is both verbal and non-verbal, as we rely not only on our ears but also on our eyes in speech perception. Another form of interaction between sight and sound happens because light travels faster than sound. In this regard, it has been observed that "visual and auditory signals of an event that reach an observer at the same point in time tend to become perceptually bound, even when the sources of those signals could not have occurred together".[101]

However, the sense of sight interacts not only with hearing but also with the other senses such as the sense of touch, also referred to as the "somatosensory system". The somatosensory system is of great interest here, first because it exemplifies the limitations of the traditional count of five senses. The concept of "somatosensory" is wider than that of touch, as etymologically it means the sensation of the body.[102] This sensation obviously involves more complex tasks and explains why, unlike the other four senses whose receptors are localised in compact sense organs (the ears for hearing, the eyes for sight, the nose for smell), the "receptors for touch and its kindred senses are distributed all over the skin and inside the body".[103] This means that the somatosensory system has the largest sensory organ, which "responds to the most diverse set of sensory stimuli, including mechanical, thermal, and chemical stimuli".[104] These stimuli provide a great variety of information, including information on the following: movement of body parts (proprioception), temperature (thermosensation), and touch (cutaneous mechanosensation), as well as pain (nociception), itch (pruriception) and the sense of internal organ function (interoception).[105] Because of these multiple tasks, the somatosensory system has also been found to be "unique among the sensory systems in that it must convey information to the central nervous system (CNS) about both external and internal sensory environments".[106]

The overall complexity of the somatosensory system increases through its interaction with other senses. For vision, for instance, it has been found that the brain connects the perception of purely visual stimuli with the perception of stimuli that "imply tactile and proprioceptive information".[107] Another experiment to simulate this phenomenon is the "rubber hand illusion", in which subjects experience an artificial hand as part of their own body because of parallel sensations of seeing and feeling their own hidden hand and a fake rubber hand being stroked at the same time.[108] The combination of the two senses creates the impression of the fake hand being one's own hand – a phenomenon that might be extended to hand-held electronic devices today. As a brief summary, the complementary relationship between the visual sense and touch was beautifully explained by the following sentence:

> The somatosensory system provides information concerning the world inside our body, whereas the visual system tells us about the outside world in which our body is located and moves.[109]

There is also an important aspect of this for the future of technology, as the sense of touch has already begun to play an important role through new technologies in a great variety of fields, such as robotic and virtual surgery, tactile alert signals (e.g. to waken a drowsy driver), and tactile product design (products that "feel" good), to mention but a few.[110] In fact, there are already many applications, products or experiences in which tactile and multisensory perception plays a crucial role, and the number and usages of these are only likely to increase in the future.

Similar interactions, both confusion and mutual reinforcement, have also been reported with regard to smell and taste. This comes as no surprise, given that the perception of flavour has been called the "most multisensory of our everyday experiences" and that sensory experiences are all based on complex multisensory interactions that rely on the integration of cues from all of the human senses.[111] For instance, the taste of black coffee may be disliked due to its bitterness while the smell of coffee is considered pleasant. A similar phenomenon can be experienced with the durian fruit and numerous other foods from around the world. Moreover, this shows the relevance of context, as the same foul odour can be pleasant "if attributed to cheese, but unpleasant if attributed to decaying meat".[112] Thus, smells and tastes can also be confused, but most of all this proves that "tastes and odours interact in the mouth to produce taste enhancement and suppression effects".[113] Similar associations have also been found for taste and flavour, as well as sound or musical notes.[114] For olfaction and vision, a similar kind of confusion has been detected in "change blindness" or the "incapacity to notice quite significant stimulus alterations".[115] In this context the finding that subliminal smells exercise "a profound influence on human behavior and perception"[116] is also interesting.

The problem of the confusion of the senses is further complicated by the fact that each of the senses permits the supra- and the subliminal reception of information. Moreover, it has been established that "information from one sense has the potential to influence how we perceive information from another, a process called multimodal perception".[117] This is also of great relevance not only to conscious perception but also to perception at the subliminal level of the individual senses alone. Even for each of the individual senses, various forms of subliminal perception have been found to exist.

To begin with, subliminal perception is thus not only limited to cases of vision, such as the tachistoscope, or sound, such as in backward masking. There are now numerous examples of the use of subliminal olfactory advertising techniques in the field of scent marketing. Scent marketing was known in ancient times, but today it is often realised by way of "air design", which describes the process of "designing fragrances and installing scent dispensing systems for scent marketing".[118] In this regard, it has also been confirmed that "perfumed sales rooms contribute to increase sales".[119] Besides, the development of technologies in the realm of smell, such as electronic noses ("e-noses"), goes back a long time and has great promise for their application not only in the food sector (e.g. to monitor the quality of food products) but also in the field of medicine.[120]

Although less explored, subliminal taste, or so-called "gustatory" sensation, and its responses in the human brain, has also been studied. Here, however, it has been concluded that, for a more complete understanding of subliminal taste processing, further studies are necessary, notably on "various subliminal taste qualities, intensities, and valences, in addition to the influence of other senses, such as somatosensation".[121] The importance of this will increase further, as new technologies known as electric taste interfaces or "e-tongues" (i.e. electrical tongue actuator stimulation devices) will eventually make it possible to produce different sensations electronically. Electronic taste sensors are already being used to ensure the acceptability of medicines to patients based on their taste.[122] However, future developments are likely soon to allow people "to experience taste digitally across the Internet as we experience text, audio and visuals online".[123]

Similar studies have been done with regard to the haptic sense and subliminal touch. For instance, in experiments conducted in two restaurants, it was found that waitresses who lightly and unobtrusively touched diners on the hand or shoulder received higher tips.[124] In another study, the objective was to find out whether subliminal haptic stimuli are capable of affecting human preferences towards those stimuli, and this was confirmed by the results.[125] As subliminal haptic cues have been found to have an impact on decision-making, these considerations can also be applied in the design of various objects, with particular relevance for the "design of packaging, textile, wall covers, clothing for comfort, and overall any touchable environment".[126] Further possible applications mentioned are in "the context of complex task performance when instead of instructions, preferred properties can be assigned to the desired object/interface/handle etc.".[127] This will also open further fields of application through "interaction in VR [virtual reality] and in remote telemanipulation applications".[128] Like the other senses, touch or haptic sensations are being developed via "e-skin", which denotes "an electronic device that can mimic and reproduce various properties of human skin through a combination of materials and structural designs and, therefore, has profound implications for smart robotics, the Internet of Things (IoT), and human–machine interfaces".[129]

Based on the findings regarding subliminal perception by each of the senses in isolation, it is interesting to note that the individual senses have been found not only to interfere with each other but also to reinforce the experience altogether. This finding confirms the importance of multisensory experiences, and also has great practical relevance for the economy of today and tomorrow. Generally, the economy has seen a gradual transformation from the tangible to the intangible nature of economic offerings, which has been captured by the notions of the creative economy.[130] In law, the rise of intangible aspects has been recognised by the evolution of the multilateral trading system, from trade in goods, to trade in services, and, notably, to the inclusion of intellectual property rights in trade. The same trend is set to persist, and intangible cognitive aspects can be expected to play an even greater role in the so-called "experience economy", which refers to the transition from selling traditional goods and services to selling experiences by wrapping them around traditional economic offerings with a view to selling them better. It was in this context that a multisensory experience was highlighted as an important instrument for businesses, as summarised in the finding that "the more sensory an experience, the more memorable it will be".[131]

The principal idea behind engaging several or all of the senses is to enhance the customer experience, which eventually translates into returning customers and higher profits. Examples include hair stylists applying shampoo and lotions "not simply for styling reasons but because they add more tactile sensations to the customer experiences".[132] Equally, casinos add fragrances, on the basis of studies that have identified an increase in revenues from slot machines in areas exposed to a pleasant aroma.[133] Similar findings have also been made in the field of packaging design, where multisensory aspects can enhance both marketing and the customer experience.[134] An interesting example of subliminal perception in this area is the characteristics of the typeface of brand names, which can set specific expectations in the mind of the viewer; for example, the roundness of the *Spencerian Script* used for the Coca-Cola logo on bottles becomes associated with the presence of a sweet-tasting drink.[135] A study on conscious and unconscious priming has shown that "masked brand logos (e.g., logo of McDonald's) have the power to prime their brand names (e.g., 'McDonald's') and, remarkably, words associated to the brand".[136] Even subliminal messages of colour have been found to provide "an instantaneous method for conveying meaning and message in brand designs".[137]

The potential downside of enhancing the sensory experience to make it more memorable is that it may also lead to "addiction by design", as has been shown to exist for gambling machines.[138] Links between the design and behavioural addiction are also discussed in the context of social network sites and "nomophobia" ("no mobile phone phobia").[139] The plans for a virtual metaverse have also been found to build on addiction, as the leaked "Facebook Papers" revealed.[140]

There is no doubt that there are many more interactions between the senses, subliminally, consciously and potentially also supra-, trans- or even "paraliminally", and that many of these may be of extreme importance for judging reality in the best possible way. Very good practical examples of those sensory interactions and related illusions are found in aviation medicine.[141] In aviation, these illusions create "a sensory conflict between what the pilot sees on the instruments and what the pilot feels", which requires a decision about which sense to rely on.[142]

Overall, the role and the interactions of the senses have also given rise to many philosophical and scientific debates about a possible hierarchy between the senses.[143] In view of these manifold forms of interactions between the different senses, it is meaningless to try to establish a strict hierarchy between them. It is more the context that determines a possible primacy of one sense over another, in the same way as different art forms appeal to different senses, like the visual arts to the eyes, music to the ears, and the plastic arts to somatosensation. However, most art forms combine two or more senses or even involve all of them, as reflected in the German concept of *Gesamtkunstwerk*. The term can be translated as "total work of art" and was first coined by the German philosopher Karl F.E. Trahndorff to describe the aspiration, common to all arts, to integrate, in a way that corresponds to the unity of their inner life.[144] More recently, its meaning was aptly explained as follows:

> Translated as "the total work of art," the Gesamtkunstwerk in art theory and aesthetics refers to the synthesis of the different art forms such as singing, dancing, poetry, painting, sculpture, and architecture, as well as the multi-sensory and deeply immersive experience that a "total" performance provides.[145]

In a timeless manner, the aspirations to create a "total work of art" also live on in the time of AI and robotics, in the form of contemporary media art or the *Robot Opera* (2015), a "robotic opera for eight semi-autonomous robot performers".[146]

Nevertheless, in the context of the complex interactions between the senses, it is also essential to recall the following two points related to the hierarchy of the senses:

> The hierarchy of the senses is both a cultural construction (and therefore based on ideological premises) and a product of the phylogenetic development of the human species (upright physical posture, species–specific increase in the performance of the brain) and the technological changes that have taken place in the course of the process of civilisation (displacement of an oral culture by one that is written, the invention of printing, etc.).[147]

The role of human (cognitive) evolution and technological changes especially deserves to be highlighted as these two factors seem not only to be closely related but also to be of great relevance to the present context of the regulation of AI. The evolution of technology has always been closely intertwined with human evolution.[148] Externally, this entwinement was highlighted by Jean Baudrillard's characterisation of technologies as the mind's extension of the body.[149] Accordingly, telescopes and microscopes become extensions of the eyes, vehicles extensions of human locomotion, and even medical technologies extensions of vital internal functions of the body, such as a respirator representing the lungs, or a pacemaker the heart.[150] Many of these health devices are now also upgraded to use AI (e.g. the "Internet of Medical Things") to enhance the human body: examples are smart pacemakers, smart socks (i.e. baby monitors), artificial valves, brain and spine electric stimulators, or computerised artificial limbs, which create further risks.[151] Responses to the Covid-19 pandemic have further accelerated the use of AI, the IoT, big data and advanced analytics technology, as well as machine learning.[152]

The natural tendency of humans to consider artificial things that are external to them as a part of them was experimentally proved by the rubber hand illusion.[153] Thus, AI can indeed be seen as an extension of the human mind, which fits well with the characterisation of AI as a mimic of the human mind. The mimicry gives rise to a paradox, but will eventually cover both conscious and unconscious aspects of cognition.[154] It also fits with the analogy of a black box to describe the secret processes both in the brain and in the computer.[155] In turn, even computers are now described as having a "subconscious"[156] or even as using "subliminal channels".[157] Like the human mind, these intelligent machines can also be manipulated and misled by the use of adversarial images and even audio.[158] The conceptualisation of technologies as extensions of the human body also resonates with the general idea of *homo faber*, which the Roman writer Appius Claudius Caecus described as someone who is able to shape her or his own destiny (*Homo faber suae quisque fortunae*).[159] Suiting the case of AI very well, the term *homo faber* was also used by Henri Bergson to define intelligence as "the faculty of manufacturing artificial objects".[160]

These analogies are by no means one-way paths from the mind to the tool. They equally invite the question of how these novel "tools" or "toys", like the computer, digital technology, artificial intelligence and augmented reality, will cognitively affect the senses and perception in the future mind.[161] The future of the senses is perhaps currently best captured by the notion of synaesthesia, meaning enhanced interaction and greater unity between the senses. In technical terms, synaesthesia can be seen as the original desire underlying augmented reality, which can be seen as the extension of the sense organs in the future. These analogies also function as important reminders that there should be a public debate not only about how technologies externalise important traits of the human existence but also about how we, in turn, seek ways of internalising them.

Furthermore, the parallel trends in the evolution of human intelligence and that of artificial intelligence as visible in technology are also reflected in changes in language.[162] The analogy between language and technology is reflected in the parallel convergence of technologies, the use of portmanteau words and oxymora in language, and the joint consideration of the senses. The same analogy extends to law by virtue of the proposed regulation of AI, as language, through engineering metaphors, influences both the study and the design of technologies.[163] More generally still, language, and particularly metaphors, is seen as a manifestation of the connections between technology and the human mind.[164] Not surprisingly, language has in the same way been found to influence the law, as "law changes as language changes – perhaps because language changes".[165] In turn, it has also been proved that law does not always lag behind technological change but is itself capable of transforming technology (often through change in language in general and metaphors in particular).[166] This dual role of law was well explained in the following words:

> Technical advances frequently bring considerable pressure to bear on the law to adjust. But this also applies the other way around. Of course the law influences technology and technological advance. The law is simultaneously an enabler and a limiting factor for technology.[167]

Another example of the influential role of language is provided by science fiction. Science fiction, an apparent oxymoron, has proved its great value in forecasting the future. It is possibly also a way of predicting the future by creating it. Fiction and science fiction can be regarded as providers of both supra- and subliminal cues, which may well influence their readers and, if placed intentionally, also give their authors – by way of predictive programming – the power to predict the future.[168] For example, George Orwell's dystopian science fiction novel *Nineteen Eighty-Four* predicted, in 1948, that

> [T]he invention of print, however, made it easier to manipulate public opinion, and the film and the radio carried the process further. With the development of television, and the technical advance which made it possible to receive and transmit simultaneously on the same instrument, private life came to an end.[169]

In hindsight, Orwell's novel already ceased to be science fiction in 1984, and now belongs to the "science of (legal) history".

Ultimately, history too is, or ought to be, about the future.[170] So is law, which also makes frequent use of its own kind of fictions, those known as "legal fictions".[171] For the present purpose and given that senses evolve over time, it is therefore also useful to consider what kind of new senses may develop in the future, according to science fiction writers. According to them, new senses will include X-ray vision, a mind-reading sense, a sixth sense (the ability to perceive the future), infrared perception, a sense that can analyse the composition of objects (Terminator's perception), and the ability to perceive danger (Spider-Sense), to mention but a few.[172] This marks a valid approach, as technological inventions often follow the inspiration of science fiction writers like Jules Verne and H.G. Wells, referred to as "nostalgic visionaries", who predicted modern technology by the power of their imagination often long before it was actually realised.[173] For instance, Wells formulated the idea of a "world brain", which fits the analogy of aspirations to use AI and big data to play the role of an omniscient being.[174] The brain has also been compared to the computer (and vice versa)[175] and the internet.[176] This also matches the idea of humans playing God, by way of "Google as God" or a "digital crystal ball".[177] Reflected in the term *homo deus*, humans playing God can also be seen – fitting the time of the Anthropocene[178] – as the time at which we should not blame catastrophes and failures on nature or God, but instead recognise that it is "within our power to make things better and to reduce the incidence of suffering even further".[179]

The mysterious line between (scientific) fact and fiction is also blurred in the mind, as Niklas Luhmann noted with regard to information received from scientific media and fictitious entertainment industries.[180] A similar effect may also be at work in the mind when it comes to the distinction between past and future, given that the understanding and perception of time itself may change drastically in the future.[181] Interestingly, "time" has also been identified as the missing dimension of the psychophysics of subliminal perception.[182] Here big data and AI (externally) and psychophysics and synaesthesia (internally) may be regarded as the combined effort by technology and cognition to realise Laplace's hypothetical Demon as an omniscient being able to predict future events.[183]

In sum, these observations seem to support the hypothesis that the human state of awareness termed "consciousness" is a very complex process involving the senses, brain, and mind. In this regard, a binary separation between nonconscious and conscious processing is found to be too simplistic.[184] This is also known as the mind–body (or mind–brain) problem.[185] Consciousness therefore remains a paradox, as does the human brain.[186] Paradoxes generally not only represent "instances where current knowledge may be deficient" but also "enable true 'paradigm shifts' in certain areas of scientific inquiry".[187] Decisively, they also highlight the need for more holistic and dynamic thinking, summarised as "oxymoronic thinking".[188] Applied to consciousness, such thinking must be based on a multisensory approach to perception. This is especially true because "multisensory processes are at play in almost everything we do".[189] This is also confirmed in the following quote:

> Our eyes, ears, nose, tongue and skin provide an interface for the brain to interact with the world around us. While there is simplicity in covering each sensory modality independently, *we are organisms that have evolved the ability to process multiple modalities as a unified experience.*[190]

With regard to the cognitive process underlying a unified experience, there is a need to explore a greater unity of the senses, a kind of "common sense" that integrates the activity of several senses.[191] This is also important in the present context, in which the techniques deployed by AI systems may operate on two or more senses at the same time. In line with a unified multisensory experience, such an operation may also happen in a combined way, in which information is received subliminally in one or more senses and supraliminally in the remaining ones. This phenomenon in perception is captured by "synaesthesia", which provides – metaphorically and actually – a useful point of departure for a greater integration of the senses.

The joint consideration of the senses has emerged in the notion of synaesthesia, which literally means "to sense together". It has been defined as "a condition in which one sensory modality also gives rise to a sensation in a different modality".[192] Synaesthesia has also been described as a "neurological blending of the senses",[193] "sensory blending",[194] or a "hidden sense".[195] It has also been stated that in synaesthesia a "sensory stimulation (or even imagining an inducer) can elicit an additional concurrent experience (or its mental representation)", which allows synaesthetes to "see sounds, smell words, taste colours, or feel tactile shapes when tasting food".[196] In line with the unlimited number of senses, synaesthesia has for a long time been known to be experienced in a variety of forms.[197] At this time, more than fifty forms of synaesthetic perception have been categorised.[198] Some of the most common categories are "grapheme-colour synaesthesia" (when a person sees colours when viewing letters, numbers, or words) and "lexical–gustatory synaesthesia" (when a person experiences flavours upon hearing certain words).[199]

Synaesthesia is often falsely regarded as a "neurological defect", and synaesthetes treated as "patients". In fact, everyone experiences synaesthesia, for instance when reading literature with "metaphors in which terms relating to one kind of sense-impression are used to describe sense-impressions of other kinds".[200] Synaesthesia even plays a crucial role in decision-making.[201] Thus the synaesthetic experience is likely to be common to everyone but to vary in the number and kinds of senses or perhaps in intensity. There is also scientific evidence that suggests that all of us are born as synaesthetes,[202] or even that if one is not born with that ability, one can be trained in it.[203] Synaesthesia therefore marks a multisensory process, which corresponds to most of our daily experiences. From an evolutionary perspective, the gene(s) involved in synaesthesia have been said to conceal a "hidden agenda", one that may hint at the direction of the future development of the senses or the emergence of a new sense organ.[204]

For this reason it is critical to stress that synaesthesia has now become accepted by the medical community as an absolutely real phenomenon and has been received with growing interest in many more disciplines, including but not limited to "neurology, psychology, linguistics, comparative anatomy, artistic creativity, philosophy, and the mind–body problem".[205] As will be shown, it has also received great attention in law and, notably, in legal semiotics.[206] For present purposes, it can be stated that research into this phenomenon has confirmed what Merleau-Ponty wrote in 1962:

> *Synaesthetic perception is the rule*, and we are unaware of it only because scientific knowledge shifts the centre of gravity of experience, so that we have unlearned how to see, hear, and generally speaking, feel, in order to deduce, from our bodily organization and the world as the physicist conceives it, what we are to see, hear and feel.[207]

Overall, synaesthesia is a real-life phenomenon and a perfect metaphor for the unity of the senses. It is a suitable concept for the discussion of AI systems that deploy subliminal techniques beyond consciousness. In the past, the invention of cinematography was compared to synaesthesia, as cinema was called "the only aesthetic language suited to the post-industrial, post-literate, man-made environment with its multidimensional simulsensory network of information sources".[208] Moreover, the evolution of cinema, from silent movies to sound and then to 3D, 4D, and even 5D movies shows a clear trend towards the greater integration of the senses. AI systems will carry this process even further in the near future.

For the regulation of AI, the fundamental question of the standards for a possible violation of the prohibition of subliminal techniques will ultimately hinge upon the thresholds drawn both for each of the individual senses and for all of them jointly. This is the principal question, namely what kind of information passes beneath the limits of human perception, which means that it would be perceived subliminally. Here the principal problems are, first, that each of the senses is assumed to have a different threshold. A second problem relates to the criteria that are used for establishing thresholds of perception, such as light or speed for vision or molecules for sound and smell.[209] This is reflected in the controversy regarding the effect of images screened at a speed beyond 24 frames per second, as reflected in the notorious "25th" frame, which is often held to form the threshold between the sub- and the supraliminal perception of images.[210] Moreover, some information can be assessed by two different senses: "the skin can be used for sound localization with accuracy nearly as good as that for hearing".[211] What, then, are the thresholds for hearing,[212] smelling,[213] tasting,[214] or touch[215]? It appears impossible to determine such thresholds for each of these senses. To give but one more reason, the thresholds for all senses seem to change when we age.[216]

These questions are no doubt of great practical relevance to both technology and the law. For the application of hearing thresholds in technology, for instance, it is possible to list a number of applications for tools operating beyond our hearing, such as ultrasonic washing machines, intruder alarms, ultrasonic animal repellers, and automatic door-openers.[217] For the other senses, the same questions exist or will arise when electric skins, tongues, and noses and other novel devices become widely available. Many more products operating beyond the thresholds of the other senses may also be of interest and find useful applications in future products, such as the use of pheromones for pest control or the development of non-bitter medicines.[218]

The question about thresholds falls within the field of psychophysics, where efforts to establish absolute thresholds of the senses, that is, to divide the states of unconsciousness and consciousness, go back a long time.[219] These efforts usually expose individuals to progressively stronger stimuli to find the minimum stimulus that the person detects 50% of the time.[220] However, the problem with such absolute thresholds is that they do not exist, as some people are more sensitive than others and even the same person experiences different thresholds at different times.[221] This explains why the idea of thresholds has been largely discounted.[222] In sum, the problem of absolute sensory thresholds has been aptly summarised as follows:

> Unfortunately, even after stimulus characteristics are taken into account, there is no absolute threshold that can be universally recommended: thresholds for a given stimulus vary both intra- and interpersonally. *One method of handling such variability is to set thresholds uniquely for each individual.*[223]

In the legal realm, this finding makes it difficult to prohibit subliminal techniques, because of the impossibility of drawing a universal line of distinction between awareness and non-awareness. In this context, it has also been noted that perceptual awareness cannot be regarded as a unitary concept, because "perceptual input often consists of various aspects, each with their own thresholds for awareness".[224] The interaction between the senses creates an additional problem, namely that a person may not detect a haptic stimulus but may see that someone has tried to touch her/him, or does not taste that food is bad but does smell it. Furthermore, studies have also shown that perceptual sensitivity is altered by the integration of multiple sensory cues.[225]

This means that subliminal techniques are relevant not only for each of the individual senses but also for the sum of their mutual combinations. This also leads to a problematic conclusion that, even if absolute thresholds could be established for each sense individually, there remains the serious problem of the distinction between subliminal and conscious perception for all the senses jointly. In this regard, the mind is pretty fickle, as it may register a certain stimulus but still choose for some reasons to ignore it, as is the case with the perception of our noses.[226] Like an "open secret", to use another oxymoron, some things become invisible because they are always there. A similar observation has been made for olfaction: it was found that "although human odorant detection thresholds are very low, only unusually high odorant concentrations spontaneously shift our attention to olfaction".[227]

In law, the impossibility of establishing absolute thresholds, either inter- or intra-personally, is highly problematic. A threshold could thus be established merely on the basis of a legal fiction using the mindset of an "ordinary" or "reasonable" consumer, albeit that the criteria used in such tests would also be volatile and changing.[228]

In spite of these problems regarding the taxonomy of the senses, the dichotomies of mind–body or "conscious–non-conscious", and the absence of absolute sensory thresholds, there are some useful conclusions to be drawn for the future regulation of AI systems. First, it becomes clear that the human experience has always been a multisensory process. Historically, there was a long tradition of regarding and studying the senses in isolation and giving vision and sound the greater priority among them. This stance must no longer be regarded as adequate, as notably the study of synaesthesia has shown. It means that the senses need to be studied simultaneously in isolation and in their unity. Second, it is also important to consider the constant change in the innovation of new technologies, as it is foreseen by virtue of Article 4 AIA. It is also reflected in the notion of the experience economy, which – in order to maximise profits – seeks to integrate a maximum number of senses in order to make the consumption of economic offerings more memorable. Moreover, novel technologies driven by digitisation are also catching up with regard to the other senses. Various electronic devices mimicking the human senses, such as electric skins, tongues or noses are already being developed and will complete the AI-driven creation of a multisensory augmented and virtual reality in no time.[229]

In parallel to the procedure of Article 4 AIA, it will be necessary not only to monitor and study progress in the development of AI systems but also to carry out a close and constant monitoring of changes in human cognition, as changes in the sense organs have regularly occurred throughout history. This has been confirmed and briefly mentioned in the context of the linkages between technology, language, law, and cognition.[230]

Finally, it is important to note in this context that synaesthesia provides a promising field not only for neuroscience and other scientific disciplines but also for law. In this respect, the relationship between law and the senses was described as follows:

> The question of *the relation between law and the senses necessarily touches upon the synaesthetic nature of all perception.* As law itself is not something properly observable, but is rather a principle operative through a non-circumscribable matrix of material, imaginal, and intellectual forms, so the sensing of law is unintelligible without reference to the principle of synthesis which governs sensation, that is, the common sense and sensing of sense first named by Aristotle's commentators as *synaesthesia*.[231]

Synaesthesia thus stands for the need to consider the law more closely with respect to the senses, both individually and collectively, and is also captured by the related concepts and fields covered by legal semiotics and legal synaesthesia.[232] Ultimately, present and future complex realities, including so-called "virtual realities" created by AI and learning machines, will also require broader cognitive changes, for instance in the field of logic. For law in particular, this will require the traditionally binary mode of legal reasoning to be complemented by a more flexible or multivalent legal logic.[233] If intelligent machines, an oxymoron,[234] are already able to compute with fuzzy logic and equally fuzzy words, then the law should not lag behind.[235] This is particularly true as the law itself is highly paradoxical, as was beautifully outlined by Benjamin N. Cardozo:

> These unending paradoxes tease us with the challenge of a riddle, the incitement of the chase. The law, like science generally, if it could be followed to its roots, would take us down beneath the veins and ridges to the unplumbed depths of being, *the reality behind the veil.*[236]

In a similar mode, even the law's origin has been found to be paradoxical, a feature that poses both an obstacle to and a precondition for its better understanding.[237]

Notes

1 Leonard Mlodinov, *Subliminal: How Your Unconscious Mind Rules Your Behaviour* (New York: Vintage Books, 2012) 34 and John A. Bargh and Tanya L. Chartrand, "The unbearable automaticity of being" (1999) 54 *American Psychologist* 462–479, 462.
2 Eduard Zeller, *A History of Greek Philosophy: From the Earliest Period to the Time of Socrates*, vol. II (London: Longmans, Green & Co, 1881) 267.
3 Otto Pötzl, "The relationship between experimentally induced dream images and indirect vision" (1960) 2(3) *Psychological Issues* 41–120.
4 Gary R. VandenBos (ed.), *APA Dictionary of Psychology*, 2nd ed. (Washington: American Psychological Association, 2015) 816.
5 Paul F. Lazarsfeld, "The psychological aspect of market research" (1934) 14(1) *Harvard Business Review* 54–71.
6 Ron Fullerton, "The beginnings of motivation research, 1934–1954: a prequel to Fullerton 2013" (2015) 7(4) *Journal of Historical Research in Marketing* 509–523.
7 Wilson Bryan Key, *Subliminal Seduction: Ad Media's Manipulation of a Not $o Innocent America* (New York: Signet, 1973) 21 and Paul J. Albanese, "The unconscious processing information" (2015) 15(1) *Marketing Theory* 59–78, 60.
8 James Vicary, "How Psychiatric Methods Can be Applied to Market Research" (1951) 235(6) *Printer's Ink* 39–48.
9 Vance Packard, *The Hidden Persuaders* (New York: Ig Publishing, 2007).
10 *Ibid.*, 240.
11 Anthony R. Pratkanis et al., "Is Subliminal Persuasion a Myth?" in Jason A. Nier (ed.), *Taking Sides: Clashing Views in Social Psychology* (New York: McGraw-Hill, 2007) 230–255 and Ap Dijksterhuis, Henk Aarts, and Pamela K. Smith, "The Power of the Subliminal: On Subliminal Persuasion and Other Potential Applications in Ran R. Hassin, James S. Uleman, and John A. Bargh (eds.), *The New Unconscious* (Oxford: Oxford University Press, 2005) 77–106, 79.
12 Charles Trappey, "A Meta-Analysis of Consumer Choice and Subliminal Advertising" (1996) 13(5) *Psychology & Marketing* 517–530, 519.
13 Christian Fichter, "Werbung" in Christian Fichter (ed.), *Wirtschaftspsychologie für Bachelor* (Berlin: Springer, 2018) 99–130, 114.
14 Johan C. Karremans, Wolfgang Stroebe, and Jasper Claus, "Beyond Vicary's fantasies: The impact of subliminal priming and brand choice" (2006) 42 *Journal of Experimental Social Psychology* 792–798, 797.
15 *Ibid.*
16 Eldon Taylor, "Subliminal Information Theory Revisited: Casting Light on a Controversy" (2007) 10(3) *Annals of the American Psychotherapy Association* 29–33, 29 [*Italics* added].
17 George Lakoff and Mark Johnson, *Metaphors We Live By* (Chicago: The University of Chicago Press, 1980) 3.
18 Tanya L. Chartrand and Gavan J. Fitzsimons, "Nonconscious Consumer Psychology" (2011) 21 *Journal of Consumer Psychology* 1–3, 3.
19 VandenBos, *supra* note 4, 960.
20 Sid Kouider et al., "Cerebral Bases of Subliminal and Supraliminal Priming during Reading (2007) 17 *Cerebral Cortex* 2019–2029, 2019.

21 Timothy O. McNamara, *Semantic Priming: Perspectives from Memory and Word Recognition* (New York: Psychology Press, 2005) 105.
22 R.B. Zajonc, "Attitudinal effects of mere exposures" (1968) 9(2) *Journal of Personality and Social Psychology* 1–27, 23 and R.B. Zajonc, "Mere exposure: A gateway to the subliminal" (2001) 10 *Current Directions in Psychological Science* 224–228, 227.
23 Norman F. Dixon and Susan B.A. Henley, "Personality Factors and Subliminal Perception" in Uwe Hentschel, Gudmund Smith, and Juris G. Draguns (eds.), *The Roots of Perception: Individual Differences in Information Processing within and beyond Awareness* (Amsterdam: Elsevier, 1986) 39–47.
24 Brandon Randolph-Seng and Robert D. Maher, "Does Subliminal Persuasion Work? It Depends on Your Motivation and Awareness" (2009) 33 *Skeptical Inquirer* 49–53.
25 Jeff Chester, "Cookie Wars: How New Data Profiling and Targeting Techniques Threaten Citizens and Consumers in the 'Big Data' Era" in Serge Gutwirth et al. (eds.), *European Data Protection: In Good Health?* (Dordrecht: Springer, 2012) 53–77, 53–55.
26 Dirk Helbing, "Societal, Economic, Ethical and Legal Challenges of the Digital Revolution: From Big Data to Deep Learning, Artificial Intelligence, and Manipulative Technologies" (2015) *arXiv:1504.037516–7* [*Italics* added]; https://arxiv.org/abs/1504.03751.
27 Wolfgang Reitberger et al., "Ambient Persuasion in the Shopping Context" in Jörg Müller, Florian Alt, and Daniel Michelis (eds.), *Pervasive Advertising* (London: Springer, 2011) 309–323, 310 and 322.
28 Dave Lakhani, *Subliminal Persuasion: Influence & Marketing Secrets They Don't Want You To Know* (Hoboken, NJ: John Wiley & Sons, 2008) 2 and Erin J. Strahan, Steven J. Spencer, and Mark P. Zanna, "Subliminal priming and persuasion: Striking while the iron is hot" (2002) 38 *Journal of Experimental Social Psychology* 556–568.
29 Richard H. Thaler and Cass R. Sunstein, *Nudge: Improving Decisions About Health, Wealth, and Happiness* (New Haven, CT: Yale University Press, 2008) 244.
30 Julia Puaschunder, *Behavioral Economics and Finance Leadership* (Cham: Springer, 2020) 166.
31 Michael Guihot, Anne F. Matthew, and Nicolas P. Suzor, "Nudging Robots: Innovative Solutions to Regulate Artificial Intelligence" (2017) 20(2) *Vanderbilt Journal of Entertainment & Technology Law* 385–456, 385.
32 Dirk Helbing et al., "Will Democracy Survive Big Data and Artificial Intelligence?" in Dirk Helbing (ed.), *Towards Digital Enlightenment: Essays on the Dark and Light Sides of the Digital Revolution* (Cham: Springer, 2019) 73–98, 76.
33 Thomas Bohrmann, "Werbung" in Christian Schicha and Carsten Brosda (eds.), *Handbuch Medienethik* (Wiesbaden: Springer, 2010) 293–303, 294.
34 Nathaniel Klemp, "When Rhetoric Turns Manipulative: Disentangling Persuasion and Manipulation" in Wayne Le Cheminant and John M. Parrish (eds.), *Manipulating Democracy: Democratic Theory, Political Psychology, and Mass Media* (London: Routledge, 2011) 59–86, 64–65.

35 Mihail C. Roco and William Sims Bainbridge (eds.), *Converging Technologies for Improving Human Performance: Nanotechnology, Biotechnology, Information Technology and Cognitive Science* (Dordrecht: Springer, 2003), Peter Ludes, *Convergence and Fragmentation: Media Technology and the Information Society* (Bristol: Intellect, 2008), Sang M. Lee and David L. Olson, *Convergenomics: Strategic Innovation in the Convergence Era* (Farnham: Gower, 2010), and Michael Kackman et al. (eds.), *Flow TV: Television in the Age of Media Convergence* (London: Routledge, 2011).

36 Mohamed Elgendi et al., "Subliminal Priming – State of the Art and Future Perspectives" (2018) 8(54) *Behavioural Science* 1–23, 15; https://doi.org/10.3390/bs8060054.

37 Art. 13(2) European Convention on Transfrontier Television, *European Treaty Series – No. 132* (5 May 1989); https://rm.coe.int/168007b0d8.

38 Oliver Schaar, "Article 10 (Principles for Advertising and Teleshopping)" in Oliver Castendyk, E.J. Dommering and Alexander Scheuer (eds.), *European Media Law* (Alphen aan den Rijn: Kluwer Law International, 2008) 489–512, 509.

39 European Economic Communities, Council Directive 89/552/EEC (Television Without Frontiers Directive), OJ L 298/23–30 (17 October 1989) [TWFD].

40 Schaar, *supra* note 38, 494.

41 Directive (EU) 2018/1808 (Audiovisual Media Services Directive), OJ L 303/69–92 (28 November 2018) [*Italics* added] [AVMSD].

42 Council of Europe (CoE); https://www.coe.int/en/web/portal.

43 European Broadcasting Union (EBU); https://www.ebu.ch/home.

44 European Platform of Regulatory Authorities (EPRA); https://www.epra.org/.

45 European Advertising Standards Alliance (EASA); https://www.easa-alliance.org.

46 European Regulators Group for Audiovisual Media Services (ERGA); https://erga-online.eu/.

47 See the European Regulators Group for Audiovisual Media Services "List of regulators in the field of audiovisual media services"; https://erga-online.eu/?page_id=43.

48 Schaar, *supra* note 38, 509.

49 Email by the Rundfunk und Telekom Regulierungs-GmbH (RTR) of 22 October 2021 (on file with the author).

50 Mariacristina Reale, "Digital Market, Bloggers, and Trendsetters: The New World of Advertising Law" (2019) 8(3) *Laws* 1–14; https://doi.org/10.3390/laws8030021.

51 Article 5(9) Federal Law No. 38-FZ (13 March 2006) on advertising.

52 Advertising Law of the People's Republic of China (2021 Amendment) [CLI Code] CLI.1.5012735(EN); https://www.pkulaw.com/en_law/8ed14f353bf1e5fdbdfb.html.

53 Article 7(1) Macau Advertising Law [Law No. 7/89/M], Establishing the general regime of advertising activities, Official Bulletin No. 36/1989 (4 September 1989); https://bo.io.gov.mo/bo/i/89/36/lei07.asp.

54 Advertising Standards Council of India (ASCI), "The Code for Self-Regulation of Advertising Content in India"; https://ascionline.in/images/pdf/code_book.pdf.

55 The Advertising Standards Council of India (ASCI), "The Guidelines For Influencer Advertising in Digital Media"; https://asci.social/guidelines.
56 Article 5 of the International Chamber of Commerce (ICC), "ICC Advertising and Marketing Communications Code" (International Chamber of Commerce, 2018); https://iccwbo.org/content/uploads/sites/3/2018/09/icc-advertising-and-marketing-communications-code-int.pdf.
57 Nicholas Hirshon, "A "Great Power" Defended and Denounced: An Examination of Twentieth-Century Advertising and Advertising Criticism in the United States" (2020) 46(3) *Journalism History* 265–283.
58 Mark Bartholomew, *Adcreep: The Case Against Modern Marketing* (Stanford, CA: Stanford Law Books, 2017) 117.
59 Laura R Salpeter and Jennifer I Swirsky, "Historical and Legal Implications of Subliminal Messaging in the Multimedia: Unconscious Subjects" (2012) 36(3) *Nova Law Review* 497–520, 502–504.
60 §52 of Section 15 of the Federal Trade Commission Act of the United States; http://uscode.house.gov/view.xhtml?req=granuleid%3AUSC-prelim-title15-chapter2-subchapter1&edition=prelim.
61 §55 (a) (1) of Section 15 of the Federal Trade Commission Act of the United States, *ibid.*
62 Omer Lee Reed Jr, "The Psychological Impact of TV Advertising and the Need for FTC Regulation" (1975) 13(2) *American Business Law Journal* 171–184, 174.
63 Elena Paraskevas-Thadani, "Banning the Thought: Saving the Lungs of Children by Banning Subliminal Messages in Tobacco Advertisements" (1997–1998) 2 *Syracuse Journal of Legislation and Policy* 133–164, 140.
64 Bartholomew, *Adcreep, supra* note 58, 117.
65 Federal Trade Commission (FTC), "Advertising FAQ's: A Guide for Small Business"; https://www.ftc.gov/tips-advice/business-center/guidance/advertising-faqs-guide-small-business.
66 Federal Trade Commission (FTC), "Advertising and Marketing"; https://www.ftc.gov/tips-advice/business-center/advertising-and-marketing.
67 Olivia Goodkin and Maureen Ann Phillips, "The Subconscious Taken Captive: A Social, Ethical, and Legal Analysis of Subliminal Communication Technology" (1981) 54(5) *Southern California Law Review* 1077–1140, 1077.
68 Chi-Ru Jou, "The Peril of a Mental Association Standard of Liability: The Case against the Subliminal Confusion Cause of Action" (2006) 11 (1) *Virginia Journal of Law & Technology* 1–43, 4–9.
69 Steven H Hartman, "Subliminal Confusion: The Misappropriation of Advertising Value" (1988) 78(4) *The Trademark Reporter* 506–522, 507–508.
70 Goodkin and Phillips, *supra* note 67.
71 Harry Schiller, "First Amendment Dialogue and Subliminal Messages" (1982) 11(2) *New York University Review of Law and Social Change* 331–362, 331 and 336.
72 Scot Silvergate, "Subliminal Perception and the First Amendment: Yelling Fire in a Crowded Mind" (1990) 44(5) *University of Miami Law Review* 1243–1282, 1243.
73 Schiller, *supra* note 71, 346.

74 *Ibid.*, 348.
75 Christopher C. French, *Paranormal Perception: A Critical Review* (London: The Institute for Cultural Research, 2006) 4.
76 David Matsumoto (ed.), *The Cambridge Dictionary of Psychology* (Cambridge: Cambridge University Press, 2009) 624.
77 *Ibid.*
78 Juliet Dee, "Subliminal Lyrics in Heavy Metal Music: More Litigation, Anyone" (1994) 16(3) *Communications and the Law* 3–24, 3.
79 *Ibid.*
80 Select Committee on Intelligence, *Project MKUltra, the CIA's Program of Research in Behavioural Modification* (Washington: U.S. Government Printing Office, 1977); see also Jaron Harambam, *Contemporary Conspiracy Culture: Truth and Knowledge in an Era of Epistemic Instability* (Abingdon, Oxon: Routledge, 2020) 17–18.
81 Howard L Wolk, "You Won't Know It When You See It: An Essay on Subliminal Communication and First Amendment Theory" (1990) 23(4) *Columbia Journal of Law and Social Problems* 523–550, Richard Fitzer, "Do Ozzy Osbourne and Judas Priest Contribute to the Market Place of Ideas?" (1991) 1(1) *DePaul Journal of Art, Technology & Intellectual Property Law* 2–11, Pamela Marsden Capps, "Rock on Trial: Subliminal Message Liability" (1991) 1 *Columbia Business Law Review* 27–50, Dee, *supra* note 78, and Nicole Grattan Pearson, "Subliminal Speech: Is It Worthy of First Amendment Protection" (1995) 4(3) *Southern California Interdisciplinary Law Journal* 775–806.
82 Matthew W. Daus, "Subliminal Messages in Music: Free Speech or Invasion of Privacy" (1992) 9(2) *University of Miami Entertainment And Sports Law Review* 241–296, 245.
83 Saurabh Malgaonkar et al., "An AI Based Intelligent Music Composing Algorithm: Concord" (2013) *International Conference on Advances in Technology and Engineering (ICATE)* 1–6; https://doi.org/10.1109/ICAdTE.2013.6524723.
84 Charles S. Areni and David Kim, "The Influence of Background Music on Shopping Behavior: Classical Versus Top-Forty Music in a Wine Store" (1993) 20 *NA – Advances in Consumer Research* 336–340.
85 Lindsay M. Timmerman et al., "A Review and Meta-Analysis Examining the Relationship of Music Content with Sex, Race, Priming, and Attitudes" (2008) 56(3) *Communication Quarterly* 303–324, 320.
86 Robert F. Bornstein, Dean R. Leone, and Donna J. Galley, "The Generalizability of Subliminal Mere Exposure Effects: Influence of Stimuli Perceived Without Awareness on Social Behavior" (1987) 53(6) *Journal of Personality and Social Psychology* 1070–1079, 1076.
87 R.B. Zajonc, "Mere exposure", *supra* note 22, 225.
88 J.J.C. Smart, "Sensations and Brain Processes" (1959) 68(2) *The Philosophical Review* 141–156, 142.
89 Katrina G. Geddes, "Ocularcentrism and Deepfakes: Should Seeing Be Believing?" (2021) 31(4) *Fordham Intellectual Property, Media and Entertainment Law* 1042–1083, 1042.
90 Fiona Macpherson, "Taxonomising the Senses" (2011) 153(1) *Philosophical Studies: An International Journal for Philosophy in the Analytic Tradition* 123–142.

91 Jon Driver, Martin Eimer, and Emiliano Macaluso, "Cross-Modal Consequences of Human Spatial Attention" in Laurent Itti, Geraint Rees, and John K. Tsotsos (eds.), *Neurobiology of Attention* (Amsterdam: Elsevier, 2005) 187–196, 187, Iiro P. Jääskeläinen, *Introduction to Cognitive Neuroscience* (London: Bookboon.com, 2012) 86, and Lars Kjelldahl, *Multimedia: Systems, Interaction and Applications* (Berlin: Springer-Verlag Berlin, 1992) 41.

92 Raghunath Tiruvaipati, *Information Theory of the Cosmos: How the New Science of Information Changes Our Understanding and Perception of the Universe* (New Delhi: Educreation, 2018) 37.

93 Lionel Bently, "Introduction" in Lionel Bently and Leo Flynn (eds.), *Law and the Senses: Sensational Jurisprudence* (London: Pluto Press, 1996) 3.

94 Noam Sagiv, Roger T. Dean, and Freya Bailes, "Algorithmic Synesthesia" in Roger T. Dean (ed.), *The Oxford Handbook of Computer Music* (Oxford: Oxford University Press, 2009) 294–311, 294.

95 Harry McGurk and John MacDonald, "Hearing Lips and Seeing Voices" (1976) 264 *Nature* 746–748, 746.

96 Geoffrey Beattie, *Visible Thought: The New Psychology of Body Language* (London: Routledge, 2004) 1.

97 Yannis M. Assael et al., "LIPNET: End-to-End Sentence Level Lipreading" (2016) *arXiv:1611.01599* 1–13, 1; https://arxiv.org/abs/1611.01599.

98 Neil Midgley, "New technology catches Hitler off guard" *The Telegraph* (22 November 2006); https://www.telegraph.co.uk/news/uknews/1534830/New-technology-catches-Hitler-off-guard.html.

99 Ya Zhao, Rui Xu, and Mingli Song, "A Cascade Sequence-to-Sequence Model for Chinese Mandarin Lip Reading" (2019) *arXiv:1908.04917* 1–6, 1; https://arxiv.org/abs/1908.04917.

100 Christopher S. Milligan, "Facial Recognition Technology, Video Surveillance, and Privacy" (1999) 9(1) *Southern California Interdisciplinary Law Journal* 295–334, 333.

101 Derek H. Arnold, Alan Johnston and Shinya Nishida, "Timing sight and sound" (2005) 45 *Vision Research* 1275–1284, 1284.

102 Ernest Klein, *A Comprehensive Etymological Dictionary of the English Language* (Amsterdam: Elsevier, 1966) 1472.

103 Carl Sherman, "The Senses: The Somatosensory System" *Dana Foundation* (12 August 2019); https://dana.org/article/the-senses-the-somatosensory-system/.

104 Luo, Liqun, *Principles of Neurobiology*, 2nd ed. (Boca Raton, FL: CRC Press, 2021) 260.

105 *Ibid.*

106 Randall J. Nelson, "Preface" in Randall J. Nelson (ed.), *The Somatosensory System: Deciphering the Brain's Own Body Image* (Boca Raton, FL: CRC Press, 2001).

107 Kaspar Meyer et al., "Seeing Touch Is Correlated with Content-Specific Activity in Primary Somatosensory Cortex" (2011) 21 *Cerebral Cortex* 2113–2121, 2121.

108 M.P.M. Kammers et al., "The rubber hand illusion in action" (2009) 47 *Neuropsychologia* 204–211, 204.

109 William H. Edwards, *Motor Learning and Control: From Theory to Practice* (Belmont, CA: Wadsworth, 2011) 76.
110 Alberto Gallace and Charles Spence, *In Touch with the Future: The Sense of Touch from Cognitive Neuroscience to Virtual Reality* (Oxford: Oxford University Press, 2014) 203, 234, and 250.
111 Charles Spence, "Multisensory Flavor Perception" (2015) 161 *Cell* 24–35, 24.
112 Paul Rozin, "'Taste-smell confusions' and the duality of the olfactory sense" (1982) 31(4) *Perception &Psychophysics* 397–401, 397.
113 Richard J. Stevenson, John Prescott and Robert A. Boakes, "Confusing Tastes and Smells: How Odours can Influence the Perception of Sweet and Sour Tastes" (1999) 24(6) *Chemical Senses* 627–635, 633.
114 Anne-Sylvie Crisinel and Charles Spence, "As bitter as a trombone: Synesthetic correspondences in nonsynesthetes between tastes/flavors and musical notes" (2010) 72(7) *Attention, Perception, & Psychophysics* 1994–2002.
115 Richard J. Stevenson, "Olfactory illusions: Where are they?" (2011) 20 *Consciousness and Cognition* 1887–1898, 1894–1895.
116 Lee Sela and Noam Sobel, "Human olfaction: a constant state of change-blindness" (2010) 205 *Experimental Brain Research* 13–29, 13.
117 Adam J. Privitera, "Sensation and perception" in Robert Biswas-Diener and Edward Diener (eds.), *Noba Textbook Series: Psychology* (Champaign, IL: DEF publishers, 2021); http://noba.to/xgk3ajhy.
118 Bernadette Emsenhuber, "Scent Marketing: Making Olfactory Advertising Pervasive" in Jörg Müller, Florian Alt, and Daniel Michelis (eds.), *Pervasive Advertising* (Springer, 2011) 343–360, 344.
119 *Ibid.*
120 M. Ghasemi-Varnamkhastia et al., "Potential application of electronic nose technology in brewery" (2011) 22(4) *Trends in Food Science & Technology* 165–174, 168 and Erica R. Thaler and C. William Hanson, "Medical applications of electronic nose technology" (2005) 2(5) *Expert Review of Medical Devices* 559–566, 559.
121 Camilla Arndal Andersen et al., "EEG discrimination of perceptually similar tastes" (2019) 97 *Journal of Neuroscience Research* 241–252, 252.
122 Abeer H.A. Mohamed-Ahmed et al., "Non-human tools for the evaluation of bitter taste in the design and development of medicines: a systematic review" (2016) 21(7) *Drug Discovery Today* 1170–1180, 1179.
123 Adrian David Cheok and Kasun Karunanayaka, *Virtual Taste and Smell Technologies for Multisensory Internet and Virtual Reality* (Cham: Springer, 2018) 2.
124 Diane Ackerman, *A Natural History of the Senses* (New York: Vintage Books, 1990) 122–123.
125 Marcos Hilsenrat and Miriam Reiner, "The impact of subliminal haptic perception on the preference discrimination of roughness and compliance" (2011) 85 *Brain Research Bulletin* 267–270, 269.
126 *Ibid.*, 270.
127 *Ibid.*
128 *Ibid.*, 420.
129 Chunfeng Wang, Caofeng Pan, and Zhonglin Wang, "Electronic Skin for Closed-Loop Systems" (2019) 13 *ACSNano* 12287–12293, 12287.

130 John Howkins, *The Creative Economy: How People Make Money From Ideas* (London: Penguin, 2002) xiii–xiv.
131 B. Joseph Pine II and James H. Gilmore, *The Experience Economy: Work is Theatre & Every Business a Stage* (Boston: Harvard Business School Press, 1999) 59.
132 *Ibid.*
133 Lana Lam, "Casinos get a whiff of dollars and scents: a nose for business, or just fragrant exploitation?" *South China Morning Post (Hong Kong)* (1 May 2011) 1.
134 Carlos Velasco and Charles Spence, "Multisensory Product Packaging: An Introduction" in Carlos Velasco and Charles Spence (eds.), *Multisensory Packaging: Designing New Product Experiences* (Cham: Palgrave Macmillan, 2019) 1–18, 4.
135 Carlos Velasco and Charles Spence, "The Role of Typeface in Packaging Design" in Carlos Velasco and Charles Spence (eds.), *Multisensory Packaging: Designing New Product Experiences* (Cham: Palgrave Macmillan, 2019) 79–101, 81.
136 Gigliola Brintazzoli, "Conscious, but not unconscious, logo priming of brands and related words" (2012) 21 *Consciousness and Cognition* 824–834, 824.
137 Faten Farouk Atrees, "The concept of subliminal messages in Brand design" (2013) 3(1) *International Design Journal* 23–28, 26.
138 Natasha Dow Schüll, *Addiction by Design: Machine Gambling in Las Vegas* (Princeton, NJ: Princeton University Press, 2012) 14.
139 Eliana Bergamin, *Social network sites addiction by design: a compatibilist free-will analysis towards policy intervention* (Master Thesis) (Enschede: University of Twente, 2021) 24 and 31; http://purl.utwente.nl/essays/88302.
140 Raf Casert and Kelvin Chan, "Facebook whistleblower warns that metaverse will be 'addictive'" *WDSU News* (9 November 2021); https://www.wdsu.com/article/facebook-whistleblower-warns-that-metaverse-will-be-addictive/38200565#.
141 Jorg Draeger and Jürgen Kriebel (eds.), *Praktische Flugmedizin* (Landsberg: ECOMED, 2002) 82–83.
142 Federal Aviation Administration (FAA), *Spatial Disorientation*, 4; https://www.faa.gov/pilots/safety/pilotsafetybrochures/media/SpatialD.pdf.
143 Danijela Kambaskovic-Sawers and Charles Wolfe, "The Senses in Philosophy and Science: From the Nobility of Sight to the Materialism of Touch" in Herman Roodenburg (ed.), *A Cultural History of the Senses in the Renaissance* (London: Bloomsbury, 2019) 107–125.
144 Karl F.E. Trahndorff, *Aesthetik oder Lehre von der Weltanschauung und Kunst* (Berlin: Maurer, 1827) 312.
145 Sylvia J. Martin, "Michael Jackson's Gesamtkunstwerk: Artistic Interrelation, Immersion, and Interactivity: From the Studio to the Stadium" (2015) 11(5) *Liminalities: A Journal of Performance Studies* 1–34, 2.
146 Wade Marynowsky, Julian Knowles, and Andrew Frost, "Robot Opera: A Gesamtkunstwerk for the 21st Century" in Jeffrey T.K.V. Koh et al. (eds.), *Cultural Robotics* (Cham: Springer, 2016) 143–158.
147 Robert Jütte, *A History of the Senses: From Antiquity to Cyberspace* (Cambridge: Polity, 2005) 61 [footnote omitted].

148 Sarah Kaplan and Mary Tripsas, "Thinking about technology: Applying a cognitive lens to technical change" (2008) 37 *Research Policy* 790–805.

149 Jean Baudrillard, *Symbolic Exchange and Death* (Los Angeles: SAGE, 1993) 178.

150 Regis A. De Silva, "End-of-Life Legislation in the United States and the Semiotics of the Female Body" in Sarah Earle, Carol Komaromy, and Caroline Bartholomew (eds.), *Death and Dying: A Reader* (London: Sage, 2009) 25–33, 27.

151 Linda F. Hogle, "Enhancement Technologies and the Body" (2005) 34 *Annual Review of Anthropology* 695–716 and Nicole M. Thomasian and Eli Y. Adash, "Cybersecurity in the Internet of Medical Things" (2021) 10(3) *Health Policy and Technology* 1–9.

152 Raju Vaishya et al., "Artificial Intelligence (AI) applications for COVID-19 pandemic" (2020) 14 *Diabetes & Metabolic Syndrome: Clinical Research & Reviews* 337–339; https://doi.org/10.1016/j.dsx.2020.04.012 and Nishita Mehta and Sharvari Shukla, "Pandemic Analytics: How Countries are Leveraging Big Data Analytics and Artificial Intelligence to Fight COVID-19?" (2022) 3(54) *SN Computer Science* 1–20; https://doi.org/10.1007/s42979-021-00923-y.

153 Gallace and Spence, *supra* note 110, 183–185.

154 Eugene Piletsky, "Consciousness and Unconsciousness of Artificial Intelligence" (2019) 11 *Future Human Image* 66–71, 70; https://doi.org/10.29202/fhi/11/7.

155 Bernice B. Donald and Erica Bakies, "A Glimpse inside the Brain's Black Box: Understanding the Role of Neuroscience in Criminal Sentencing" (2016) 85(2) *Fordham Law Review* 481–502, 501–502; and Frank Pasquale, *The Black Box Society: The Secret Algorithms that Control Money and Information* (Cambridge, MA: Harvard University Press, 2015).

156 Robert C. Schank, "The Computer's Subconscious" (2008) 23(3) *Applied Artificial Intelligence* 186–203, 190 and 203.

157 Alexander Hartl et al. "A Subliminal Channel in EdDSA: Information Leakage with High-Speed Signatures" (2017) *MIST '17: Proceedings of the 2017 International Workshop on Managing Insider Security Threats* 67–78, 67; https://doi.org/10.1145/3139923.3139925.

158 Yehao Kong and Jiliang Zhang, "Adversarial Audio: A New Information Hiding Method and Backdoor for DNN-based Speech Recognition Models" (2019) *arXiv* 1–12, 3; https://arxiv.org/abs/1904.03829.

159 Gaius Sallustius Crispus, *Coniuratio Catilinae Et Bellum Jugurthinum* (Venice: Aldus, 1563) 95 and Henryk Hoffmann, *Latin in Modern Fiction: Who Says It's a Dead Language?* (Wilmington, DE: Vernon Press, 2021) 261.

160 Henri Bergson, *Creative Evolution* (New York: Henry Bolt, 1911) 139.

161 Lorenzo Cecutti, Anthony Chemero and Spike W. S. Lee, "Technology may change cognition without necessarily harming it" (2021) 5 *Nature Human Behaviour* 973–975, 974–975.

162 Rostam J. Neuwirth, "The 'Letter' and 'Spirit' of Comparative Law in the Time of 'Artificial Intelligence' and other Oxymora" (2020) 26(1) *Canterbury Law Review* 1–31, 8.

163 Maarten Boudry and Massimo Pigliucci, "The mismeasure of machine: Synthetic biology and the trouble with engineering metaphors" (2013) 44

Studies in History and Philosophy of Biological and Biomedical Sciences 660–668.

164 Douwe Draaisma, *Metaphors of Memory: A History of Ideas about the Mind* (Cambridge: Cambridge University Press, 2000) 3.

165 Adolph S. Oko, "Introduction" in Nathan S. Isaacs, *The Law and the Change of Law* (Miami, FL: Hardpress, 2012) 1–8, 6.

166 Lyria Bennett Moses, "Recurring Dilemmas: The Law's Race to Keep up with Technological Change" (2007) 2007(2) *University of Illinois Journal of Law, Technology & Policy* 239–286, 239 and Wolfgang Däubler, "Gestaltung neuer Technologien durch Recht?" (1986) 19(2) *Zeitschrift für Rechtspolitik* 42–48, 42.

167 Volker Boehme-Neßler, *Pictorial Law: Modern Law and the Power of Pictures* (Berlin: Springer, 2011) 7.

168 Rostam J. Neuwirth, "The Regulation of 'Fake News' in the Time of Oxymora: Facts and Fictions about the Covid-19 Pandemic as Coincidences or Predictive Programming?" (2021) *International Journal for the Semiotics of Law* 1–27, 12; https://doi.org/10.1007/s11196-021-09840-y.

169 George Orwell, *1984* (New York: Signet, 1950) 156.

170 Barbara Adam, "History of the future: Paradoxes and challenges" (2010) 14(3) *Rethinking History* 361–378, 373.

171 Lon L. Fuller, *Legal Fictions* (Stanford, CA: Stanford University Press, 1967) 1 and Kristin Y. Albrecht, *Fiktionen im Recht* (Baden: Nomos Verlag, 2020).

172 Fiona Macpherson, "Individuating the Senses" in Fiona Macpherson (ed.), *The Senses: Classical and Contemporary Philosophical Perspectives* (Oxford: Oxford University Press, 2011) 3–43, 21–22.

173 Timothy Unwin, "Technology and Progress in Jules Verne, Or Anticipation in Reverse" (2000) 93(1) *Journal of the Australasian Universities Language and Literature Association* 17–35, 18 and 31.

174 Herbert G. Wells, *World Brain* (San Bernardino, CA: Read Books Ltd, 2016) 16 and Francis Heylighen and Marta Lenartowicz, "The Global Brain as a model of the future information society: An introduction to the special issue" (2017) 114 *Technological Forecasting & Social Change* 1–6, 1.

175 John Von Neumann, *Computer and the Brain* (New Haven, CT: Yale University Press, 1958) and Bruce J. Berman, "Artificial Intelligence and the Ideology of Capitalist Reconstruction" (1992) 6 *AI & Society* 103–114, 110.

176 Naomi Goldblum, *The Brain-Shaped Mind: What the Brain Can Tell Us about the Mind* (Cambridge: Cambridge University Press, 2004) 5–6.

177 Dirk Helbing, *Next Civilization: Digital Democracy and Socio-Ecological Finance—How to Avoid Dystopia and Upgrade Society by Digital Means*, 2nd ed. (Cham: Springer, 2021) 63–84.

178 Eckart Ehlers and Thomas Krafft, "Managing Global Change: Earth System Science in the Anthropocene" in Eckart Ehlers and Thomas Krafft (eds.), *Earth System Science in the Anthropocene* (Berlin: Springer, 2006) 5–12, 5.

179 Yuval Noah Harari, *Homo Deus: A Brief History of Tomorrow* (New York: Harper, 2017) 19–20.

180 Niklas Luhmann, *The Reality of Mass Media* (Stanford, CA: Stanford University Press, 2000) 58.

181 Carlo Rovelli, *The Order of Time* (New York: Riverhead Books, 2018) 4.
182 Matthew Hugh Erdelyi, "Subliminal perception and its cognates: Theory, indeterminacy, and time" (2004) 13 *Consciousness and Cognition* 73–91, 81.
183 Pierre-Simon Laplace, *Philosophical Essay on Probabilities* (New York: Springer, 1995) 2, Richard Shearmur, "Dazzled by data: Big Data, the census and urban geography" (2015) 36(7) *Urban Geography* 965–968, 965 and Julia Simner, Neil Mayo, and Mary-Jane Spiller, "A foundation for savantism? Visuo-spatial synaesthetes present with cognitive benefits" (2009) 45 *Cortex* 1246–1260, 1255.
184 Stanislas Dehaene et al., "Conscious, preconscious, and subliminal processing: a testable taxonomy" (2010) 10(5) *TRENDS in Cognitive Sciences* 204–211, 208.
185 Colin McGinn, "Can We Solve the Mind–Body Problem?" (1989) 98 (391) *Mind* 349–366, 366 ("The answer to the question that forms my title is therefore 'No and Yes'.") and Iona Miller "On the Quantum Aspects of Brain-Mind Problem" (2014) 5(3) *Scientific GOD Journal* 201–215, 201.
186 Narinder Kapur (ed.), *The Paradoxical Brain* (Cambridge: Cambridge University Press, 2011).
187 Narinder Kapur et al., "The Paradoxical Nature of Nature" in Narinder Kapur (ed.), *The Paradoxical Brain* (Cambridge: Cambridge University Press, 2011) 1–13, 1.
188 Rostam J. Neuwirth, *Law in the Time of Oxymora: A Synaesthesia of Language, Logic and Law* (New York: Routledge, 2018) 253.
189 Andrew J. Bremner, David J. Lewkowicz, and Charles Spence, "The multisensory approach to development" in Andrew J. Bremner, David J. Lewkowicz and Charles Spence (eds.), *Multisensory Development* (Oxford: Oxford University Press, 2012) 1–26, 18.
190 Privitera, *supra* note 117 [*Italics* added].
191 Lawrence E. Marks, *The Unity of the Senses: Interrelations among the Modalities* (New York: Academic Press, 1978) 3.
192 Noam Sagiv, "Synesthesia in Perspective" in Lynn C. Robertson and Noam Sagiv (eds.), *Synesthesia: Perspectives from Cognitive Neuroscience* (Oxford: Oxford University Press, 2005) 3–10, 3.
193 VandenBos, *supra* note 4, 1060.
194 Ophelia Deroy, *Sensory Blending: On Synaesthesia and Related Phenomena* (Oxford: Oxford University Press, 2017).
195 Cretien van Campen, *The Hidden Sense: Synesthesia in Art and Science* (Cambridge, MA: The MIT Press, 2007) 158.
196 Aleksandra Maria Rogowska, *Synaesthesia and Individual Differences* (Cambridge: Cambridge University Press, 2015) 1.
197 Raymond Holder Wheeler, *The Synaesthesia of a Blind Subject* (Eugene, OR: University of Oregon Press, 1920) 3.
198 Richard E. Cytowic, *Synesthesia: A Union of the Senses*, 2nd ed. (Cambridge, MA: MIT Press, 2002) 17.
199 VandenBos, *supra* note 4, 1060.
200 Shane Butler and Alex Purves, "Introduction: Synaesthesia and the Ancient Senses" in Shane Butler and Alex Purves (eds.), *Synaesthesia and the Ancient Senses* (Abingdon, Oxon: Routledge, 2014) 1–7, 1.

201 Raymond Holder Wheeler and Thomas D. Cutsforth, "Synaesthesia in Judging and Choosing" (1928) 1(3–4) *The Journal of General Psychology* 497–519.

202 Daphne Maurer, Laura C. Gibson, and Ferrinne Spector, "Infant Synaesthesia: New Insights into the Development of Multisensory Perception" in Andrew J. Bremner, David J. Lewkowicz, and Charles Spence (eds.), *Multisensory Development* (Oxford: Oxford University Press, 2012) 229–250 and Ophelia Deroy and Charles Spence, "Are we all born synaesthetic? Examining the neonatal synaesthesia hypothesis" (2013) 37 *Neuroscience & Biobehavioral Reviews* 1240–1253.

203 Nicolas Rothen, Andrea-Laura Wantz, and Beat Meier, "Training synaesthesia" (2011) 40 *Perception* 1248–1250 and Roger Walsh, "Can Synaesthesia Be Cultivated? Indications from Surveys of Meditators" (2005) 12(4–5) *Journal of Consciousness Studies* 5–17.

204 David Brang and V. S. Ramachandran, "Survival of the Synesthesia Gene: Why Do People Hear Colors and Taste Words?" (2011) 9(11) *PLoS Biology* 1–6, 5.

205 Richard E. Cytowic, *Synesthesia: A Union of the Senses* (New York: Springer-Verlag, 1989) 2.

206 Sarah Marusek (ed.), *Synesthetic Legalities: Sensory Dimensions of Law and Jurisprudence* (Abingdon, Oxon: Routledge, 2017) and Neuwirth, *Law in the Time of Oxymora, supra* note 188.

207 Maurice Merleau-Ponty, *Phenomenology of Perception* (London: Routledge & Keagan Paul, 1962) 229 [*Italics* added].

208 Gene Youngblood, *Expanded Cinema* (New York: P. Dutton & Co., 1970) 77.

209 R.A. Weale, "The Absolute Threshold of Vision" (1955) 35(1) *Physiological Reviews* 233–246, 233.

210 Maria Florea, "History of the 25th Frame. The Subliminal Message" (2016) 6(3) *Communication and Globalization International Journal of Communication Research* 261–266.

211 George, A. Gescheider, "Some Comparisons Between Touch and Hearing" (1970) *IEEE Transactions on Man-Machine Systems* 28–35, 28.

212 L.J. Wheeler and E.D.D. Dickson, "The Determination of the Threshold of Hearing" (1952) 66(8) *The Journal of Laryngology & Otology* 379–395.

213 G.H. Cheesman and Stella Mayne, "The influence of adaptation on absolute threshold measurements for olfactory stimuli" (1953) 5(1) *Quarterly Journal of Experimental Psychology* 22–30.

214 L.M. Bartoshuk, "The psychophysics of taste" (1978) 31(6) *The American Journal of Clinical Nutrition* 1068–1077.

215 Carl E. Sherrick and James C. Craig, "The Psychophysics of Touch" in William Schiff and Emerson Foulke (eds.), *Tactual Perception: A Sourcebook* (Cambridge: Cambridge University Press, 1982) 55–81.

216 Belinda Train, *Introduction to Psychology: Fresh Perspectives* (Cape Town: Pearson, 2007) 122.

217 Kaoru Ashihara et al., "Hearing threshold for pure tones above 20 kHz" (2006) 27 *Acoustical Science and Technology* 12–19, 12.

218 Peter Witzgall, "Pheromones - future techniques for insect control?" (2001) 24(2) *Pheromones for Insect Control in Orchards and Vineyards IOBC wprs Bulletin* 114–122 and Mohamed-Ahmed et al., *supra* note 122, 1170

219 John A. Swets, "Is there a sensory threshold?" (1961) 134 *Science* 168–177, 168.
220 Spencer A Rathus, *Psych*[6]*: Introductory Psychology* (Boston: Cengage, 2020) 64.
221 *Ibid.*
222 Jeffrey N. Rouder and Richard D. Morey, "The nature of psychological thresholds" (2009) 116(3) *Psychological Review* 655–660, 655.
223 Pamela K. Smith and Kathleen McCulloch, "Subliminal Perception" in V.S. Ramachandran (ed.), *Encyclopedia of Human Behavior*, vol. 1, 2nd ed. (London: Academic Press, 2012) 551–557, 551 [*Italics* added].
224 Stefan Wiens, "Subliminal emotion perception in brain imaging: findings, issues, and recommendations" (2006) 156 *Progress in Brain Research* 105–121, 117.
225 Jan Drugowitsch et al., "Optimal multisensory decision-making in a reaction-time task" (2014) 3 *eLife* 1–19, 1; https://doi.org/10.7554/eLife.03005.
226 Michael Pace, *Subliminal Psychology 101: How to Stealthily Penetrate, Influence, and Subdue Anyone's Mind without Them Suspecting a Thing* (Scotts Valley, CA: CreateSpace Publishing, 2018) 10–11.
227 Sela and Sobel, *supra* note 116, 13.
228 Thomas R. Lee, Glenn L Christensen, and Eric D. DeRosia, "Trademarks, Consumer Psychology, and the Sophisticated Consumer" (2008) 57(3) *Emory Law Journal* 575–650, 649 and Celine Shirooni, "Native Advertising in Social Media: Is the FTC's Reasonable Consumer Reasonable" (2018) 56 *Washington University Journal of Law & Policy* 221–240, 222.
229 Susan S. Schiffman and Tim C. Pearce, "Introduction to Olfaction: Perception, Anatomy, Physiology, and Molecular Biology" in Tim C. Pearce et al. (eds.), *Handbook of Machine Olfaction: Electronic Nose Technology* (Weinheim: WILEY-VCH Verlag, 2003) 1–31, 26 and Wang, Pan, and Wang, *supra* note 129.
230 Michael Polanyi, *Knowing and Being* (Chicago: University of Chicago Press, 1969), 148, Arthur Zajonc, *Catching the Light: The Entwined History of Light and Mind* (Oxford: Oxford University Press, 1993), 184, and Neuwirth, *Law in the Time of Oxymora, supra* note 188, 135–43.
231 Nicola Masciandaro, "Synaesthesia: The Mystical Sense of Law" in A Philippopoulos-Mihalopoulos (ed.), *Routledge Research Handbook on Law and Theory* (London: Routledge, 2018), 179–201, 180 [*Italics* added].
232 Rostam J. Neuwirth, "Legal Semiotics and Synaesthesia" in Anne Wagner and Sarah Marusek (eds.), *Research Handbook on Legal Semiotics* (Cheltenham: Edward Elgar, forthcoming in 2023), Rostam J. Neuwirth, "International Adjudication and Semiotics" in Hélène Ruiz Fabri (ed.), *Max Planck Encyclopedia of International Procedural Law (MPEiPro)* (Oxford: Oxford University Press, 2021) 1–30.
233 John Dewey, "Logical Method and Law" (1924) 10(1) *Cornell Law Quarterly* 17–27, 27, Oren Perez, "Law in the Air: A Prologue to the World of Legal Paradoxes" in Oren Perez and Gunther Teubner (eds.), *Paradoxes and Inconsistencies in the Law* (Oxford: Hart, 2006) 3–38, H. Patrick Glenn and Lionel D. Smith (eds.), *Law and the New Logics*

(Cambridge: Cambridge University Press, 2017), Valentin Jeutner, *Irresolvable Norm Conflicts in International Law: The Concept of a Legal Dilemma* (Oxford: Oxford University Press, 2017) 151–153, and Neuwirth, *Law in the Time of Oxymora, supra* note 188, 230.

234 Alcibiades Malapi-Nelson, *The Nature of the Machine and the Collapse of Cybernetics: A Transhumanist Lesson for Emerging Technologies* (Cham: Palgrave Macmillan, 2017) 100.

235 Lotfi A. Zadeh, "Fuzzy Logic = Computing with Words" (1996) 4(2) *IEEE Transactions on Fuzzy Systems* 103–111, 110.

236 Benjamin N. Cardozo, *The Paradoxes of Legal Science* (New York: Columbia University Press, 1928) 134 [*Italics* added].

237 Yoav Kenny, "'Not Mutually Exclusive': Derrida and Agamben Read Kafka's '*Before the Law*'" in Agata Bielik-Robson and Adam Lipszyc (eds.), *Judaism in Contemporary Thought: Traces and Influence* (New York: Routledge, 2014) 116–126, 118.

3 The future regulation of subliminal AI systems

The preceding chapters first discussed the legal context and some preliminary critiques of the AIA's prohibition of an "AI system that deploys subliminal techniques beyond a person's consciousness". The discussion then proceeded to a brief overview of present and future AI systems that already make use of such subliminal techniques or will do in the future. To highlight some of the challenges that are expected to be caused by the planned prohibition, a broader picture of the role of subliminal perception in law was drawn by reference to the prohibition of subliminal advertising and other reported relevant cases. Finally, the matter of subliminal perception required us to take a closer look at the functioning of the senses individually and collectively, as presented under the notion of synaesthesia. In sum, the findings of these discussions allow a few preliminary conclusions to be drawn about the proposed AIA. However, they also invite a more transdisciplinary scientific debate about the implications of both the regulation of AI in general and the planned prohibition of subliminal techniques in particular. For these reasons it is now possible to revisit and make a critical assessment of the planned prohibition of subliminal AI in a more complete frame.

A The prohibition of subliminal techniques in AI systems, revisited

As a first important finding, the EU's initiative launched in April 2021 specifically to regulate AI, in a comprehensive manner and in close connection with other related existing and planned legal instruments, must be welcomed. The reason is that most of the commentators on AI cited throughout this book, from a vast field of different legal, non-legal, and scientific backgrounds, concur on the absolute necessity of regulating AI. The same necessity was meanwhile confirmed for the whole of Europe by the publicised plans of the Council of Europe's

DOI: 10.4324/9781003319436-4

Ad Hoc Committee on Artificial Intelligence (CAHAI) to pursue the regulation of AI by elaborating a regulatory framework for it. Its confirmation for the whole world was manifest in the broad consensus displayed in the adoption by the UNESCO members on 22 November 2021 of the Recommendation on the Ethics of Artificial Intelligence, which, however, is legally non-binding. Although the UNESCO Recommendation does not explicitly mention subliminal techniques, it emphasises the profound positive and negative impacts of AI, particularly on the human mind.

A second finding is that the planned prohibition of the use of AI systems that deploy subliminal techniques is likely to constitute a key aspect of the entire AIA. This provision is important because it updates the law after decades of technological advances in the fields of neuroscience and related technologies used by AI or in combination with AI. In this regard, too, experts from different scientific disciplines widely agree that the intrusive nature of these technologies is capable of directly controlling the mind, manipulating human behaviour and causing serious harm in various forms. Evidently there exist positive uses of subliminal AI, but these were not extensively discussed here. They include, for example, subliminal techniques used for self-help or (musical) therapy to counter various forms of addiction, obesity, anxiety or phobias.[1] However, even within such beneficial usages doubts often remain and controversies persist, although more recent studies have confirmed the effectiveness of therapeutic subliminal stimuli.[2] The underlying problem lies in the technology paradox, which states that any technology is per se neither bad nor good; it is usually what it is used for that makes the difference. Thus the same (subliminal) technique can be used to teach and learn, with the help of intelligent tutoring systems, or to manipulate, in the form of dark patterns or propaganda.[3] The line drawn between a beneficial and a harmful effect is therefore – as we know from the so-called "poison paradox" formulated by Paracelsus centuries ago[4] – generally very thin. It is precisely for this reason that the explicit reference to subliminal techniques in the AIA is important, because it helps to ensure that both potentially beneficial and potentially harmful usages are detected and subsequently developed (in the former case) or restricted (in the latter case). In the same way, it also confirms the need for binding laws regulating AI and controlling subliminal techniques, as ethical principles alone will not be able to deter the harmful development and use of these novel technologies.

More generally, the concrete and symbolic relevance of the subliminal in the context of AI and new technologies was well summed up by the description of "subliminal intervention" as "the primary novel paradigm of autonomic computing, next to its claimed self-awareness".[5] Hence, the explicit reference to subliminal perception must be regarded as an important step in the protection of the human right to freedom of thought and personal mental privacy, as a way to maintain an environment free from manipulation and harmful interference with a person's control over her own mind. These real dangers are aptly summarised in the following quote:

> Despite questions concerning its effectiveness, subliminal communication technology poses serious threats to the rights of individual autonomy and personal privacy. Because of the sanctity traditionally afforded these rights in our society, their loss is arguably not outweighed by possible social benefits accruing from the use of subliminal technology. Therefore, legal protection for the interests threatened by the use of subliminal communication devices is necessary.[6]

Perhaps earlier in the twentieth century there was doubt about the effectiveness of visual subliminal stimuli on a human's behaviour. More recent scientific studies have repeatedly confirmed the impact and effectiveness of such stimuli, limited only by some additional factors such as personality or context. The strength of their impact is also a function of the length of the exposure, and in this regard unprecedented evidence was found "of the longevity and impact of subliminal messages on conscious, rational decision-making".[7] In line with various findings in the marketing context, it is also likely that the impact of subliminal stimuli will increase if more senses are involved, both sub- and supraliminally. This means, also, that the state of the individual's sensory system as a whole is relevant, as stated in the following paragraph:

> In summary, these findings show that sensory perception depends not only on the stimulation's characteristics, but also on the state of the sensory system. It is not simply the stimulation strength with respect to the detection threshold, which determines whether and how a stimulus is consciously perceived or not, but also the amplitude and phase of background rhythms, as well as behavioral/cognitive factors such as vigilance, attention, and expectation. In addition to being influenced by the state of the sensory system, *perception of sensory stimuli itself continuously modifies the same system*, hence, affecting the processing of subsequent stimuli.

> Interestingly, even when a stimulus is applied at subliminal intensities and, hence, is never detectable, the brain still responds to it, which suggests that *subliminal stimulations are also relevant for behavior and further cognitive processing.*[8]

This finding reinvigorates the analogy of technology functioning as an extension of the human body and, particularly, of AI functioning as the human mind. Thus, in the same way as *sensory stimuli continuously modify the state of the sensory system*, all novel, both present and future, technologies, commonly referred to as AI, will have a mounting impact on decision-making and life as a whole. The convergence of technologies carries this process forward to the future drastic alteration of the role of subliminal and supraliminal stimuli in our conscious and unconscious lives. Thus, the quantity, intensity, frequency, and quality of exposure to a wide range of stimuli received through different channels are a true game changer, and we can expect the effects of subliminal techniques to improve and intensify further.

This hypothesis that the impact is stronger when more senses are involved has already been confirmed in the phenomenon of "deep fakes". Such videos combine image and sound, and digitally alter a person's face or body. Compared to written "fake news", deep fakes have been found to have "a much-magnified impact", and this will be exacerbated because of the way in which "today's social media-oriented information environment interacts with our cognitive biases".[9] The longer, deeper, and wider exposure of two or more senses to subliminal stimuli will make experiences more memorable and reinforce their effectiveness altogether. Merely in how they address deep fakes, the present legal and policy architectures have been found to be not optimally designed to respond to the serious harms.[10] Logically, from the smaller scale argument to the larger one, this means that the very same laws are definitely inadequate to deal with subliminal techniques, both present ones and, most of all, future ones. In sum, ethical concerns have been voiced for some time, but questions about the impact of subliminal information on users delayed regulatory actions. Now, these concerns clearly highlight the "need of unifying approaches and conceptual frameworks" not only in research but also in legal action.[11]

Therefore, it can be concluded that the various scientific studies of present, as well as future, technologies, and the related insights gained into the mysterious workings of the brain require greater attention to be paid to the role of subliminal stimuli. While the inclusion of the prohibition per se should not be questioned, there may be a need for some clarification with regard to the chosen wording "AI system that deploys (harmful) subliminal techniques beyond a person's consciousness", in both scientific and legal terms. Looking at the scientific ones, it would be good to consult regularly with various experts from the numerous fields involved about what distinguishes subliminal from supraliminal, or conscious from subconscious, perception. It would equally be important to know how the related concepts of "transliminal" or "paraliminal" perception could fit within the present state of the scientific knowledge of perception. At the same time, it would be important to clarify the issue of the thresholds of the different senses, individually and collectively. This seems to be an important question for making judgments about whether a technique is illegal because of its "subliminal" nature. Overall, a greater consensus on the terms used must be realised, and confusing terminology must be avoided.

On a different note, it has been found that "thresholds for a given stimulus vary both intra- and interpersonally".[12] In practice, this would mean that the only way of fairly judging a possible violation of the provision would be to set thresholds uniquely for each individual in order to handle such variability. This would be impracticable, just as it would be impracticable to assess a speeding violation on the basis of the individual driver's driving skills. For these reasons, answers to these preliminary scientific questions are also of great relevance to the concrete wording of the proposed prohibition.

Moreover, there are important lessons to be learned from the past experiences with prohibitions in subliminal advertising. First, innovations in technology, particularly relating to the senses, that use various electronic devices simulating and transmitting stimuli that are not only visual and auditory but are also olfactory, gustatory, and haptic will also require advertisement laws around the world to be revisited. In other words, the focus on the "audiovisual" aspects of information is no longer enough, even for advertising alone. The greater the number of senses engaged, the broader must be the conceptual approach. The second important lesson, however, is that greater attention must be paid to the enforcement of any future regulation on AI. In this regard, the current plethora of regional and national bodies in Europe is inadequate, because their tasks are widely duplicated but they still seem to fail to monitor content for subliminal messages or to sanction any potential violations. Instead, a system is needed that avails itself of a regulatory body that is both centralised and decentralised, to give better coordination between the supranational and national, or global and local, levels. Such a combined "*glocal*" oversight is needed because many relevant technologies will be used and operate globally, while the understanding of the senses and perception often differ locally according to the specific linguistic and cultural context.[13] Such cultural differences also manifest themselves in subliminal forms.[14] The future enforcement system should also be competent, independent, and efficient, and perhaps incorporate a review mechanism for decisions taken at the first instance.[15] Moreover, it should be both consistent and flexible in the monitoring and screening of content for subliminal messages, and AI systems for subliminal techniques, given that these systems evolve rapidly. Such a body should also have vested in it the necessary AI systems equipment to detect AI systems deploying subliminal content. The use of such technology to detect the use of subliminal AI systems would certainly help to restore the present imbalance in which surveillance technologies are being used to control citizens on the one hand and to protect them on the other.

From the perspective of the prohibition of subliminal techniques, the ongoing debate about narrowing the definition of AI, suggested and apparently also already agreed to by the competent EU institutions, must be eyed critically.[16] It is in view of the trend of convergence and the rapid pace of change that prevalence should be given to broader and more inclusive regulatory approaches. This applies both to the regulation of AI in general and to the question of the prohibition of various harmful subliminal techniques. With regard to the latter, there is a need to clarify the line drawn between manipulations that operate subliminally and those that operate supraliminally, as it seems that the complexity of human perception and cognition means that perception and cognition jointly determine decision-making and changes in human behaviour. Hence, it would perhaps be better not to combine "subliminal" with "beyond a person's consciousness", as this appears confusing and contradictory. Depending on the response from scientific experts, the word "subliminal" could be replaced by "transliminal", so as to include forms of manipulation operating either at the unconscious or at the conscious level, or even at both levels of awareness at the same time.

A similar conclusion can be drawn with regard to the scope and wording of a person's "physical or psychological harm". Here too, a more holistic, inclusive, and generic phrase should be chosen that is at least in line with the WHO's definition of health as used since 1946. This can either be a simplistic reduction to "harm" alone, which courts and judges can later interpret to include forms other than physical and psychological harm, such as emotional, cultural, collective, and societal harm, as well as cognitive harm, as previously suggested.[17] This reductionist method would also be preferable in line with the changes that would need to be made to other areas of law, such as the tort system (recognising subliminal or cumulative torts), as well as to future civil liability regimes capable of addressing the wrongs caused by AI systems. However, this also requires that the scope of harm is reconsidered. An early commentary on the proposed text suggested that the scope of the provision on subliminal techniques should be widened in order to protect human autonomy and prevent the risk that AI-driven applications will "increasingly shape our individual references as well as alter the outcomes of political decision-making".[18] For this reason, the commentary also suggests widening the scope of the provisions and, in particular, removing the harm requirement altogether.[19] The reason given is as follows:

> This definition risks giving a free pass to many manipulative AI systems, because subliminal manipulation is hard to detect and because it will be difficult for an affected person to prove a causal relationship between the subliminal manipulation and the harm incurred. In other words, the high threshold risks making this important prohibition largely symbolic.[20]

There remains indeed the question of how best to refer to harm and also to make sure that major collective harms are covered. One can take the example of a rigged election in which one voter may not have been subliminally affected by personalised manipulative practices, perhaps because s/he has no social media account, and yet the same person may eventually still suffer harm from the rigged election through the manipulation of the majority of the electorate with social media accounts. This problem between individual and collective responsibility and individual and collective harm can already be seen in the debate about (mandatory) vaccination in the case of pandemics.[21]

Therefore further thought should be given to the formulation of the harm requirement, as well as to the current limitation to harm caused to "that person or another person", which should be widened so that it also covers a wider group or society as a whole. At the same time, causation should be discussed so as to address the effects of "cumulative harms" as well. These suggestions would definitely help to make sure that a wider range of existing and future manipulative systems are covered by the prohibition, and to establish a greater symmetry in the power relationship between the "manipulator" and the "manipulated".[22]

Overall, the chosen approach of focusing on AI in general, rather than splitting AI into different areas such as the medical, transport or other sectors, must also be welcomed, particularly in the context of a rapidly evolving and converging technological and industrial environment. Here, important lessons can be learned from past developments in the cultural industries, as reflected in the concentric circles model, which describes an expansive process from the centre of core cultural sectors to the periphery of the entire economy.[23] This trend has been confirmed, notably by the dynamic terminological shift from the cultural to the creative industries.[24] The transition from cultural to creative industries eventually culminated in the finding that, because any scientific or technical innovation in any industry is creative, "any industry is, therefore, potentially a 'creative industry'".[25] Eventually, this led to the emergence of the related but broader concepts of the creative and experience economy.[26] The trend of converging industries and the emergence of cross-cutting products was found to pose a regulatory challenge even before the hype about AI, as summarised here:

> Boundaries are increasingly fading among hi-tech industries (for example, the ICT) as well as among hi-touch and hi-tech industries: nutriceutics (also called the "functional food" industry), edutainment, cosmeceutics and genetics diagnostics are just a sample of the emerging convergent markets.[27]

Cutting a long story short, the notion of the creative and experience economy points to the increasing importance of cognitive elements in the future economy. Moreover, it reflects the ongoing trend of the convergence of industries, technologies, and products. This trend of convergence also calls for greater coherence and, most of all, better coordination between different laws and legal areas. This approach is supported by the following observation about the expected impacts of AI on the law as a whole:

> Although it is important to consider the legal implications of each new technology on its own, our view is that more attention should be given to the risks that are posed when new technologies, especially those that are AI-enabled, are interconnected and interact with each other in ways that can at least seem to be unfathomable.[28]

The same need for this approach is also well-exemplified by the experiences and, notably, the various risks related to a continuing trend towards greater concentration of ownership both within specific, but also across different, media.[29] This trend has been recorded both nationally and globally,[30] and also in different sectors, such as the print media, television broadcasters, film production companies, and book publishers. Soon, in every industry and with the help of AI, there will be just the "Big Five", or fewer, big players left, as the media (e.g. Time Warner, Walt Disney, News Corporation, Viacom, and Bertelsmann) and big tech companies (e.g. Google, Amazon, Apple, Facebook, and Microsoft) show.[31] The rise of major institutional investors in the financial markets foreshadow future trends for all sectors and give rise to the apparent paradox that even small ownership stakes can have major anticompetitive effects because of collective holdings in competing companies.[32] This problem of common ownership has been identified as a newly identified competition problem, which "is of significant importance but remained undetected by competition authorities for a long time".[33] These anticompetitive effects associated with common ownership have, of course, wider implications. Already within the traditional media, cross-ownership has led to the strange paradox of greater quantity in various products but less diversity in content.[34] With the help of "big tech", the new media will carry this and other paradoxes to new heights, especially when the trend of convergence spreads from traditional media to new media as well as other sectors.[35]

It has already been found that, with digital convergence, the lines that once divided the mass media, telecommunications, and computer industries have been crossed, as can be seen from multiple examples, such as software operating system companies offering phone services, phone companies providing video distribution, and TV set manufacturers becoming music and game companies.[36] The technological convergence also resulted in a greater concentration of control of media content that has led to a situation where both intermediaries and conventional news providers have assumed more powerful roles in gatekeeping and agenda setting.[37] These powers inevitably also enhance the possibility of greater mind control exercised through the different new media channels, which also appeal to the different senses, such as print media and television to the visual and radio broadcasts to the auditory senses.

Learning from past regulatory experience is therefore important. We can expect that in no time the combination of these traditional but concentrated media outlets with various personalised AI techniques and systems will carry this trend of media convergence to new industries and to all areas of life. This new reality will open unprecedented levels of "mind control" through "agenda control".[38] The same trend also translates into the likelihood that any technology will make greater use of subliminal techniques, which provides an additional argument for a wider definition of AI systems. Here, too, it can be expected that certain core technologies, such as computers and digitisation, will gradually cast their shadow over all other sectors and technologies of the economy and, most of all, over life in all its dimensions. This argument is supported by the fact that, like the creative industries, AI systems can be described as having a cross-cutting and multidimensional nature that calls for innovative, cross-sectoral, and multidisciplinary policy responses, as well as inter-ministerial action.[39] Similarly, they require better inter-agency cooperation and inter-regime coordination at the global level.[40] Consequently, a wider and more inclusive approach also improves the chance that law and policies can overcome the obsolescence of law and render it more "future-proof".[41]

However, the "future-proofing" of laws and policies means the ability to address paradoxes, such as the paradox of our times or the paradox of the convergence of industries and products and greater divergence of laws and regulations.[42] In turn, it means rethinking some of the basic foundations, including the cognitive ones, on which laws are formulated, adopted, and implemented. The reason is that AI systems will continue the trend in which the creative industries – by way of "creative destruction"[43] – disrupt entire sectors and erode the traditional meaning given to the most significant legal concepts as well as the dominant modes of reasoning. The last point is best summed up by the principle that "the choice of one excludes the other" (*expressio unius est exclusio alterius*), the interpretation of which must be scrutinised in the light of new legal logics.[44] In the case of the cultural industries it was the dual nature of their products (having both cultural and commercial aspects) that posed serious problems to their treatment in the fragmented legal regimes of international trade on the one hand and culture on the other. The nature of AI systems will carry this process to unprecedented levels at which various former dichotomies, including those distinguishing humans from machines or thought being private from being public and, will have to be reconsidered from their origin. The oxymoron of "cyborg" (cybernetic organism) also reminds us that "once upon a time, of course, the language of science did not require us to tolerate oxymorons like the living dead".[45] Today, AI has already been recognised as a game changer and as something that will have an everlasting impact in multiple areas, with much wider implications. For law, it will hence require a new thinking based on more profound analyses and a more coordinated study of various different legal regimes at all levels of governance.

Within the EU, there is already a growing awareness of the intrinsic connection between the AIA, the GDPR, the Digital Markets Act (DMA),[46] the Digital Services Act (DSA),[47] civil liability regimes and the Product Liability Directive (PLD),[48] the Unfair Commercial Practices Directive,[49] the E-Commerce Directive,[50] the Audiovisual Media Services Directive (AVMSD),[51] and the planned regulation of virtual and augmented reality, which was found to suffer "from fragmentation across sectors, players, and applications".[52] Various linkages between different laws relevant for technologies operating subliminally or, potentially, manipulating behaviour have already been established, such as between AI, big data, privacy, and unfair commercial practices.[53] However, it will not suffice to coordinate these separate laws and regulations alone. The cross-cutting nature of these technologies means that the various laws and regulations must be better coordinated and integrated and, ideally, brought under a consistent constitutional framework securing their coherence with broader areas of law, including but not limited to fundamental rights,[54] competition law,[55] tax law,[56] finance law,[57] tort law,[58] criminal law,[59] intellectual property law,[60] global trade law[61], and international law,[62] each of which already struggles alone with the disruptive effects of AI. For the EU, this necessity goes beyond a mere constitutional debate but should also include plans for a proper EU constitution.[63]

What is more, the challenges in each of these separate legal fields will be exacerbated by the ongoing convergence, increasing interconnectedness, and concentration of ownership. Therefore, all these legal fields must be brought within a constitutional system built on fundamental rights and major codifications. Most of all, they must be based on a common language and shared understanding of the objectives related to the future of AI and life. At the same time, the EU must make parallel efforts to coordinate its plans with other partners, notably China, Russia, and the US, if global efforts like those undertaken within UNESCO are to crystallise and eventually become translated into a coherent set of global laws. For the world at large, this means "constitutionalising" and not merely to "theorising" a global legal order.

Future technological innovations in AI, particularly in connection with BCIs, fMRI, big data, IoT, blockchain, robotics, eye-tracking, and other technologies, tools or applications,[64] are likely to have a snowball effect on the meaning and interpretation of existing legal concepts. Already, their effects are reflected in language changes, notably the rise of oxymora, paradoxes and portmanteau words, which must be duly taken into account. This means, in other words, that many small and almost undetectable changes in distinct areas may still have a drastic and measurable effect on the system as a whole. It means that minor changes may lead to a fundamental change in the traditional approaches and underlying assumptions – a phenomenon well-captured by the notion of "paradigm shift". For this reason, it is also necessary to have a brief look at the wider ramifications of AI systems and, notably, subliminal techniques in relation to law.

B Wider ramifications for law: towards a right to cognitive freedom

The ongoing developments in the field of AI and, notably, cognitive sciences indicate the advent of more drastic and measurable effects on the human mind, which will henceforth determine how we perceive, process, and organise life. These effects will even determine the lives of future generations. With a greater effect of technologies on humans comes a greater responsibility in law and legal science. As mentioned above, law, language, science, technology, and most other phenomena in the world share not only an origin in the mind, but also the fact that they are undergoing drastic changes in the present era.

As captured by the description of the twenty-first century as the "Age of Paradox",[65] many of these drastic changes are manifest in an encounter with profound contradictions, disturbing paradoxes, and a rising number of "oxymora", the rhetorical cousins of paradoxes.[66] In law, these oxymora give rise to a number of "legal dilemmas" that are associated with seemingly irresolvable norm conflicts.[67] This observation is supported by numerous neologisms of the same kind as artificial intelligence and related concepts that all qualify as oxymora, such as "raw data", "social media" or "virtual reality".[68] To recall, paradoxes and oxymora, called "essentially oxymoronic concepts" in homage to Walter B. Gallie's "essentially contested concepts", share the aspect that they carry varying degrees of contradictions in terms, expressed through different rhetorical figures ranging from one word to two or more sentences.[69] A sound understanding of paradoxes is, first of all, important because they have been defining our lives in all aspects, to the extent that they are found everywhere.[70] This also greatly matters to the law, where oxymora and paradoxes have been found to be on the rise and to undermine the traditional modes of dualistic legal thinking and exclusive logic.[71] Most of all, it has been stated that making sense of paradoxes is crucial for the process of shaping the future and, possibly, a better destiny.[72]

In short, these novel essentially oxymoronic concepts describe a rapidly changing technological and societal environment and also highlight the shortcomings in traditional modes of legal thinking and the limitations of many well-established legal concepts and institutional structures. One paradox that best summarises this quality is the "paradox of our times", which was outlined by David Held as follows:

> The paradox of our times can be stated simply: the collective issues we must grapple with are increasingly global and, yet, the means for addressing these are national and local, weak and incomplete.[73]

Sadly this paradox applies not only to AI but also to many more urgent global problems, not limited to the Covid-19 global pandemic, climate change, and additional problems captured by the Sustainable Development Goals (SDGs). Even the concept of "sustainable development" qualifies as an oxymoron.[74] Solving these numerous but interconnected problems and averting more disasters and cataclysms will require concerted efforts by the international community to institute a novel global legal framework. Most of all, it will require novel ideas, some of which were outlined in a scientifically fictitious account of a future global institution called "GAIA", such as combining local and global governance into "glocal governance" and complementing hierarchy by holarchy.[75] Similar ideas have been put forward regarding a future international organisation competent for AI, such as an "International Artificial Intelligence Agency" (IAIA).[76] The reason for the latter was given as follows:

> As global problems require global solutions, we propose the establishment of an international AI regulatory agency that – drawing on inter-disciplinary expertise – could create a unified framework for the regulation of AI technologies and inform the development of AI policies around the world.[77]

These proposals for a global institutional framework must be taken seriously, because AI is also predicted to have a globally disruptive effect on global affairs and international law. This also implies that, if unregulated, global AI is capable of disrupting the instruments, institutions, and concepts of a future global legal order.[78] Another reason provided for a viable framework of international regulatory cooperation in the area of AI is "to avoid the development of nationally fragmented AI policies, which may lead to international tensions".[79]

The problem of nationally fragmented policies is well known from the fragmentation of national markets for certain technical products, like DVDs, as well as the internet, through measures known as geolocation or geoblocking.[80] The same problem can be noted in national (uncoordinated) efforts in the regulation of a related problem, namely that of "fake news", which is largely pursued nationally and without considering the revival of older international instruments, like the UN General Assembly's 1953 *Convention on the International Right of Correction*.[81]

Thus, the paradox of our times is but one example of many paradoxes, which exemplifies the fact that the recorded phenomena point to deeper problems – problems whose solutions ought to be sought at the cognitive level, as recommended by George P. Fletcher in the following words:

> One would expect that unless we properly address the questions that lie at the foundation of our legal system, we will generate paradoxes and antinomies. Now that we know more precisely what these puzzles and contradictions are, we should be impelled to attack the basic jurisprudential questions with a greater sense of urgency. If we wish to avoid disabling contradictions, *we must reach a deeper understanding of the legal premises that guide our thinking*.[82]

At the same time, these paradoxes also seem to suggest a social and intellectual need for the infiltration into law "of a more experimental and flexible logic".[83] The potential benefits of such a flexible or fuzzy logic have been noted in the context of the development of AI and unconventional computing as well as computing with words.[84] These benefits of oxymora and paradoxes also apply in other areas, where they are generally said to "offer powerful opportunities to test models and conceptual frameworks, and to enable true 'paradigm shifts' in certain areas of scientific inquiry" as well as to "contribute towards a more positive, humanistic view of diverse states of the human condition".[85] There is thus no reason to exclude the possibility of similar beneficial effects in law. To exemplify this claim, it is useful to take a short look at the field of human rights in general and the right to freedom of thought in particular.

Not coincidentally, human rights are also framed as a paradox, namely that they are both "always and never universal" for the following reason:

> Human rights are paradoxical. On the one hand, human rights are transcendent. Human rights gain power and purchase because

> they are said to belong to all people no matter who they are or where they are. On the other hand, the idea of human rights conferred on us all by virtue of being human is a convenient fiction. Humans realize their rights only in particular places with particular instruments and with particular protections.[86]

In simple terms, it can be said that the true universality of human rights lies in the paradox that all humans are equal because every single one is truly unique. Another paradox is that, despite the claims to the indivisibility of human rights, the central international human rights instruments are characterised by the split of the 1948 Universal Declaration of Human Rights (UDHR) into the two 1966 international covenants – that on Civil and Political Rights (ICCPR) and that on Economic, Social and Cultural Rights (ICESCR).[87] At the European level, a similar schism on the issue of human rights occurred with the separation at birth of the twins, the EU and the Council of Europe.[88]

These few examples clearly show that novel thinking should be applied to human rights, particularly with regard to the right most closely related to AI, namely the right to freedom of thought. This right can be found across a number of international human rights instruments, such as the ICCPR, the European Convention on Human Rights (ECHR) and the Charter of Fundamental Freedoms of the EU.[89] In the version in Article 18 UDHR this right reads as follows:

> Everyone has the right to freedom of thought, conscience and religion; this right includes freedom to change his religion or belief, and freedom, either alone or in community with others and in public or private, to manifest his religion or belief in teaching, practice, worship and observance.[90]

It seems that the mention of the "right to freedom of thought" in the context of conscience and religion has somewhat overshadowed its significance in isolation. This may partly explain why the right to freedom of thought seems to have been "forgotten" and to lack practical relevance, in stark contrast to its actual significance.[91] This also resonates with the significance of the realm of thought, given that almost anything existing in the universe "can be experienced as information".[92] This matches up with the understanding that information is not merely intangible but materially "forms" the recipient of "information", in the sense of being "*in-formed*" or "*in formation*".[93] It is the same in information theory, which transformed computers and communications, where "information" is more than the mere communication of data and spans different sciences (e.g. thermodynamics, the theory of relativity, quantum mechanics, genetics, cosmology, astronomy, and quantum computing) to combine them into the hypothesis that "everything in the universe is constructed from information".[94]

All these trends, accelerated by rapid advances in neuroscience and computing, as also used by AI, explain the urgent need for a renewed interpretation of the right to freedom of information. This need was exemplified by the impact of marketing and other persuasive methods on the mind and decision-making as follows:

> It is naïve, if not absurd, to assume that marketing is, as some advocates still pretend, primarily about conveying information. From a common sense and a normative perspective, it is about changing thoughts and influencing decision-making. In principle, such means may interfere with [the] consumer's right to remain free from manipulative interventions.[95]

Moreover, as subliminal techniques have been found to be effective in various studies, these interventions can indeed be regarded as being "paradigmatic examples of infringements" of freedom of thought.[96] This finding underlines the need to revisit and reinterpret the right to freedom of information in accordance with the changes in the regulatory context. In practical terms, the reinterpretation must be met by a parallel consideration of related rights and probably a new approach altogether to the interpretation of fundamental rights. The reason is that the right to freedom of information also relates to the right to freedom of opinion and expression, as laid down in the UDHR as follows:

> Everyone has the right to freedom of opinion and expression; this right includes freedom to hold opinions without interference and *to seek, receive and impart information and ideas through any media and regardless of frontiers.*[97]

This is also where the practical role of "oxymoronic thinking", understood as a combination of methods known as "intuitive"[98], "systemic"[99], "creative"[100], and "paradoxical"[101] thinking, comes into play.[102] Put simply, oxymoronic thinking requires the consideration that different rights, such as the rights to information and to freedom of expression, do not stand in direct opposition but mutually complement each other in seeking a deeper and wider understanding of the issues at hand. It also requires particular skills to deal with the legal dilemmas caused by norm conflicts. The solution to these dilemmas means accepting the notion of a legal dilemma, but regarding it not as an irresolvable conflict between norms but instead as a mandate to seek a more inclusive and consistent solution to the problem.[103] With the advances introduced by quantum computing and other phenomena, such situations, "in which a certain kind of conduct is, as a matter of positive law, both legal and illegal at the same time", will only increase in number and significance.[104] Most legal problems are of a paradoxical kind, as aptly paraphrased by Benjamin N. Cardozo's "verdict" that the fundamental problems of law are "the reconciliation of the irreconcilable, the merger of antitheses, [and] the synthesis of opposites".[105]

The same applies to factual aspects related to AI systems, where information may be received both subliminally and supraliminally, may inform and misinform, may be factual and fictitious, and so on, at the same time. In other words, the kind of factual and legal problems that will be encountered in the future are unlikely to be successfully framed in purely dualistic terms, which is known as a method that "trades accuracy for simplicity".[106] It has already been confirmed, by rapid technological innovations, that strictly dualistic regulatory techniques, such as prohibitions or commandments, are obsolete and inadequate.[107]

Therefore, the problems are better described as "multiple-body problems", a term that usually covers the difficulties of predicting the motion of celestial bodies in their mutual influence.[108] Similarly, the regulation of (subliminal) information also stands under the influence of several fundamental rights and also the apparent tensions between the right to freedom of information and the right to freedom of expression. A third set of related fundamental rights that should be mentioned here are the right to privacy and the right to the protection of personal data. The former is broadly stipulated in a variety of charters, but the version in Article 12 UDHR guarantees that "[N]o one shall be subjected to arbitrary interference with his privacy [...]" and "[E]veryone has the right to the protection of the law against such interference or attacks". In the EU, the latter right has crystallised from the former in a long process involving several pioneering international "data protection" instruments, such as the 1980 OECD Guidelines on the Protection of Privacy and Transborder Flows of Personal Data and the 1981 Convention for the Protection of

Individuals with regard to Automatic Processing of Personal Data.[109] In the version in Article 8 of the EU Charter of Fundamental Rights the right to personal data protection reads as follows:

1 Everyone has the right to the protection of personal data concerning him or her.
2 Such data must be processed fairly for specified purposes and on the basis of the consent of the person concerned or some other legitimate basis laid down by law. Everyone has the right of access to data which has been collected concerning him or her, and the right to have it rectified.
3 Compliance with these rules shall be subject to control by an independent authority.[110]

The intrinsic links between these and additional rights (e.g. to health) [111] are evident in the notion of "mental privacy", which UNESCO's International Bioethics Committee (IBC) used in the context of novel potential risks related to neurotechnologies. In this context, it recognised that the right to privacy is tightly linked to several other rights, such as "the right to freedom with its diverse legal and ethical aspects like freedom of speech, of association, of location, of movement and space, of beliefs, thoughts and feelings, and of behavior".[112] Mental privacy is an expression of the belief that our thoughts are private and cannot be accessed from the outside, which is fundamental to our self-model.[113] However, advances in neurotechnology capable of transmitting brain data and digital data in combination or through implanted neurodevices, as well as fMRI, already allow the mind to be read and thoughts to be made publicly available. In this regard, the IBC explicitly noted the complex risks and social issues of "mind reading" made possible by the use of unexpectedly found data or their detection based on the neuroimaging of psychological states unknown to the individual, highlighting that such data are being obtained "without the consent of the individual affected or *even the awareness that such information is being taken*".[114]

In this last phrase, we can see the combined role of techniques that deploy supra- and subliminal methods. Earlier, it was also shown that perception in general relies on all five traditional senses and possibly on a few more that are as yet neither taxonomised nor known. Taken together, the deepening understanding of cognition and the brain supports the need for a comprehensive and yet consistent framework and an integrated approach to both perception and information and, as well, to fundamental rights and regulation. Perhaps in this regard a parallel can be drawn between the past fragmented classification of the senses and the present politico-legal framework. Similarly, a parallel can be drawn between recent trends of convergence in linguistics and in technological changes. In language, the trend is towards a greater use of portmanteau words (a portmanteau word is a "word packed with two meanings"[115]) such as "emoticon", which is created from "emotion" and "icon".[116] This trend also fits with the trend in essentially oxymoronic concepts, which are found when a portmanteau word combines two apparently antagonistic meanings, which transforms it into an "oxymoron". In technology, the trend is the convergence of products and industries characterising today's "network",[117] "digital",[118] "sharing",[119] "data-driven",[120] "blockchain",[121] "experience",[122] or, lastly, "creative economy",[123] to give but a few related concepts. In combination, the two trends also emerge in the realm of trademark law, in what has been called the "evident popularity of blends in brand names".[124]

In combination, these phenomena are perhaps best summed up in a general trend towards conceptual integration (or "blending"),[125] not only of language and technology but even of the senses, as captured by the term "synaesthesia". At a higher level still, this trend may be the expression of a deeper desire to find a theory of everything and eventually *even to know everything*. Now, with the promise of AI and big data, it has been said that "the information age has inspired the dream of some keen strategists that we might be able to know everything about the world ourselves, and to shape it as desired".[126] Thus, AI can be regarded as the technological extension of our brain, in the same way as augmented and virtual reality are the extensions of all the senses sensing together, as in "synaesthesia". If this is the case, it will also be necessary to rethink the role of law in our global society, along the lines of H.G. Wells's idea of a "world brain". This also entails solving the problem of how law, in terms of legal research and legal education, can adapt to these novel and unprecedented challenges. These tasks, it is argued, will pose difficult challenges, which may best be tackled by the term "legal synaesthesia".

C Legal synaesthesia: greater unity of the senses leads to greater unity of law?

If AI, as the external projection of the human mind, is going to provide humans with the tools to predict and create the future by functioning, with the help of big data, as a "digital crystal ball",[127] then it will also be necessary to rethink and reinvent the role of law. The function of law is essentially contested and regularly subject to change. However, two metaphors are helpful to elucidate this role. The first is Pierre Lepaulle's characterisation of law as a "social medicine" designed to cure and prevent the ills that have befallen or may befall society in the future.[128] A second useful metaphor is the one coined by Lon L. Fuller, which regards lawyers as "the chief architects of our legal, political, and economic order".[129] Both metaphors, it is argued here, help to give a better framing for the question of the future role of law in general and the regulation of future technologies and AI in particular. The reverse is also true, namely that the regulation of AI and new technologies will be crucial for the future of all societies on the globe, which will also impinge upon the needs for law. Thus it really seems that the present time confronts humanity with the paradox that it seems for the first time to be in a position to predict the future by creating it. This would only confirm Ludwig Wittgenstein's predictive statement that "what is thinkable is also possible".[130]

All the paradoxes related to AI, as manifest in numerous other oxymora, require a whole series of considerations to be made both individually and collectively. In this regard, the major challenge is to guarantee maximal policy coherence and legal consistency, meaning optimal coordination and interplay between different laws and regulations locally and globally. At the global level, this goal of greater consistency requires a drastic reform of the architecture of the present international legal order. Past and present difficulties with both the United Nations Organization and the World Trade Organization, however, have shown that reforms can only be carried out successfully after relevant cognitive changes have materialised.[131] It is, therefore, claimed that in order for the necessary cognitive changes for greater coherence and inclusion to materialise, a greater synthesis between the senses is required. This supports the thesis that a greater unity of the senses will lead to a more integrated perception, which will eventually also lead to a greater unity of law in both legislative and executive terms. This is precisely where the role of the merger between synaesthesia and law to create "legal synaesthesia" comes into play.

The term "legal synaesthesia" was initially used to highlight the intrinsic connections not only between all the senses but also between all of them and the law, summarised in the statement that we see, hear, feel, touch, and even taste the law.[132] At the same time, it was also used as a metaphor for a greater unity of perception, applied not only to the different senses themselves, but also to language, logic, and law.[133] The relevance of a greater unity of the senses for different areas was outlined in the following paragraph:

> The unity of the senses reveals itself in a variety of ways: in sensory processes, where the psychophysical behavior of different senses shows marked similarities; in perceptual processes, where different senses provide common information about the world and where characteristics of sensory experience resemble one another; and in cognitive processes, where verbal metaphors describe or suggest similarities among sensory phenomena.[134]

The expression of the greater unity of senses in language via verbal metaphors or so-called "synaesthetic metaphors" (like "visual hearing")[135] or "poetic oxymora"[136] provides an especially strong link to the law, which also strongly relies on language.[137] Metaphors, it has been shown, are not only a "device of the poetic imagination" but are also "pervasive in everyday life, not just in language but in thought and action".[138] This also confirms the great relevance of semiotics for the study of law and legal synaesthesia.[139] Broadly defined as "the study of signs and symbols and their use, especially in language", semiotics is, however, not limited to language. As signs are communicated through any of the known senses, semiotics can also be "applied to the analysis of patterned human communication in all its sensory modes, i.e. hearing, sight, taste, touch and smell".[140] Equally, semiotics is of great relevance to law, as most lawyerly tasks are said to involve semiotics.[141] Not surprisingly, semiotics has also been found to be of great use to consumer advertising including subliminal messages.[142]

In a nutshell, these various linkages between language, technology, and the senses also matter greatly for law, as the rule of synaesthetic perception restates. For law, the importance of the senses is equally easy to explain, as the senses play a crucial role in the "making of sense" because they "tear reality apart into vibrant morsels and reassemble them into a meaningful pattern".[143] Therefore, legal synaesthesia may provide a strong basis for both legal theory and legal practice. For theory, it provides a good approach to legal education and research. For legal practice, it has been shown that it is closely related to adjudication, that is, the process of deciding cases, where synaesthesia can be of great use in the fields of international trade law, intellectual property law, cultural property law, and the rules of (digital) evidence, to mention but a few.[144]

These qualities, it is argued, help legal synaesthesia to address the serious challenges related to AI and new technologies. First, it is submitted that legal synaesthesia best addresses the criticism that the law is "ocularcentric" (that is, centred too much on the visual sense alone).[145] Basing the law on all the senses also corresponds to the possibilities of subliminal techniques, which are primarily thought of in visual and auditory terms, but, because of novel devices such as electronic tongues, noses, and skins, are likely to be expanded into the other senses as well. In this sense, synaesthesia is akin to augmented reality, which can be seen as the technological extension of our senses.

Second, legal synaesthesia assists the law in realising a greater consistency as an efficient "cognitive de-fragmentation technique", by remedying some of the harmful effects of the fragmentation of (international) law.[146] This is of the utmost importance given that AI and its related converging technologies have been identified as cross-cutting issues. This is also supported by the need for a more interdisciplinary approach to law, as has been suggested by legal semiotics.[147] This is of particular value for AI and subliminal techniques used especially for interactive advertising which – based on far-reaching data collection, profiling, and targeting apparatus – "incorporate some of the latest developments in such fields as semantics, artificial intelligence, auction theory, social network analysis, data mining, and neuroscience".[148]

Third, legal synaesthesia responds to the need for a greater interdisciplinarity and unity of science as the result of the continuing trend towards specialisation. This trend saw the number of disciplines increase from seven, when the first universities were founded in the thirteenth century, to more than 8000 in 2012, which invites the critical conclusion that today a "great expert in a given discipline is totally ignorant in more than 7999 disciplines".[149] This resonates with the warning that the present system is out of control because "while some experts are familiar with developments in one field, such as artificial intelligence, nanotechnology, big data or genetics, no one is an expert on everything".[150] This also means that we must ensure that human intelligence is augmented by artificial intelligence and not replaced by it.[151] The safeguarding of human intelligence is crucial, as it has been found that – in contrast to the fixed set of rules governing the world of chess – the performance of AI in "a truly open-world problem devoid of rigid rules and reams of perfect historical data" is disastrous.[152] A similar finding is termed the "Moravec Paradox", which holds that computers perform better than humans in reasoning tasks but worse in those requiring sensorimotor and perception skills.[153] These findings give rise to the following, apparently well-founded, worries:

> The risk is not that AI will become smarter than us and we will delegate important decisions to it, the risk is that it is NOT smarter than us but we delegate important decisions to it.[154]

As a last example of a paradox related to AI, there is also that of complexity, aggravated by the growing amount of data.[155] Ironically, the paradox of complexity is believed both to be caused and to be solved by AI and big data.

As a fourth benefit, legal synaesthesia matches the trends in technology and language. As exemplified throughout this book, there is a trend to frame novel phenomena, like AI, by describing them as oxymora or paradoxes or so-called "essentially contested concepts". This not only indicates that the knowledge and understanding about their underlying meaning is deficient, but also highlights the limitations inherent in traditional modes of dualistic reasoning and binary logic. The fact is that, largely driven by advances in new technologies which often use fuzzy logic in their computations, new modes of logic such as multivalent logic are increasingly also being debated in the realm of law. It has been argued that "new logics may be needed that are multivalent, paraconsistent or non-monotonic and do not adhere to the classic rules of non-contradiction and the excluded middle".[156] This need to expand the traditional use of binary logic is also confirmed by the different senses and their role in perception, as expressed in synaesthetic metaphors. Here it becomes clear that a strictly binary logic is limited when it attempts to describe situations in which two or more individual senses contradict each other or mutually complement and reinforce each other. Thus, if synaesthetic perception is the rule, as Merleau-Ponty held, the mutual interaction of these senses is often multivalent in character.

As a fifth argument, legal synaesthesia opens the door to a new understanding of time as used by law. Time can be regarded as a measure of change. Change, notably when expressed in the form of the oxymoronic concept of "constant change", provides a major challenge to the law (and the rule of law), because change is constant, continuing and inevitable, and is the dominant factor in society today, which is why "no sensible decision can be made any longer without taking into account not only the world as it is, but the world as it will be".[157] Time and temporality are particularly of great relevance to experimental forms of regulation, such as sunset clauses, nudging and many more.[158] Experimental forms of regulation are set to play an especially important role in tackling the ethical challenges related to AI, as they were explicitly included in Article 53 AIA ("AI regulatory sandboxes"). In this regard, legal synaesthesia can help to bring a new understanding of law through language. Most modern languages, by distinguishing strictly between the past, the present and the future, impose restrictions on a more complete understanding of the phenomenon of time.[159] The importance of a new understanding of time can also be seen in the interpretation of related concepts as oxymora, as in terms like "time management"[160] or "space-time".[161] In this regard, synaesthesia provides a specific condition related to time in the form of "space-time synaesthesia". This condition means the experience of time units (such as months of the year) as idiosyncratic spatial forms, and has been confirmed to exist and to be helpful in mentally organising time and processing time-based information.[162] This matters, as time has also proved to be crucial for solving paradoxes and the contradictions laid down in oxymora. Time may be the missing "fourth dimension" of the perception of three-dimensional space, which the current sensory system is unable to detect.[163] William Shakespeare pointed this link out when he wrote that "[T]his was sometime a paradox, but now the *time* gives it proof".[164]

Last but not least, time is also crucial to the present case of the regulation of AI, in order to make it trustworthy and inclusive not only in the present but particularly for future generations. This is also reflected in Amara's paradoxical law, which warns that – if no appropriate action is taken now – we are likely to underestimate the transformative and even disruptive effects of future AI systems and techniques in the medium to long term.[165] To prevent this danger, the recommendation is to act immediately. This means that the AIA, the CAHAI's planned legal framework on artificial intelligence, and the UNESCO Recommendation on the Ethics of AI are well-timed, as the time to regulate AI is now.

Notes

1 Frank Ryan, *Cognitive Therapy for Addiction: Motivation and Change* (Chichester: John Wiley & Sons, 2013) 6, 53, 56 and 60, Edwin K. Yager, *Subliminal Therapy: Using the Mind to Heal* (Carmarthen: Crown House, 2011), Rania Karam et al., "Effectiveness of Subliminal Messages and Their Influence on People's Choices" (2017) 13(17) *European Scientific Journal* 262–278, 276, and Joseph F. McGuire, Adam B. Lewin, and Eric A. Storch, "Enhancing Exposure Therapy for Anxiety Disorders, Obsessive Compulsive Disorder, and Posttraumatic Stress Disorder" (2014) 14(8) *Expert Review of Neurotherapeutics* 893–910.

2 *Cf.* Timothy E. Moore, "Subliminal Self-help Auditory Tapes: An Empirical Test of Perceptual Consequences" (1995) 27(1) *Canadian Journal of Behavioural Science* 9–20, 18 and Mathias Pessiglione, "Subliminal Motivation of the Human Brain" in Stanislas Dehaene and Yves Christen (eds.), *Characterizing Consciousness: From Cognition to the Clinic* (Berlin: Springer, 2011) 175–190, 188.

3 Aaron R. Seitz and Takeo Watanabe, "Is subliminal learning really passive?" (2003) 422 *Nature* 36, 36, Pierre Chalfoun and Claude Frasson, "Subliminal Cues While Teaching: HCI Technique for Enhanced

Learning" (2011) *Advances in Human-Computer Interaction* 1–15, 13; doi:10.1155/2011/968753, and Robert F. Bornstein, "Subliminal Techniques as Propaganda Tools: Review and Critique" (1989) 10(3) *The Journal of Mind and Behavior* 231–262, 257.

4 John A. Timbrell, *The Poison Paradox: Chemicals as Friends and Foes* (Oxford: Oxford University Press, 2005) 2 and 250.

5 Mireille Hildebrandt, "Introduction: A Multifocal View of Human Agency in the Era of Autonomic Computing" in Mireille Hildebrandt and Antoinette Rouvroy (eds.), *Law, Human Agency and Autonomic Computing: The Philosophy of Law Meets the Philosophy of Technology* (Abingdon, Oxon: Routledge, 2011) 1–11, 5.

6 Olivia Goodkin and Maureen Ann Phillips, "The Subconscious Taken Captive: A Social, Ethical, and Legal Analysis of Subliminal Communication Technology" (1981) 54(5) *Southern California Law Review* 1077–1140, 1140.

7 Simon Ruch, Marc Alain Züst, and Katharina Henke, "Subliminal messages exert long-term effects on decision-making" (2016) 2016(1) *Neuroscience of Consciousness* 1–9, 1.

8 Burkhard Pleger and Arno Villringer, "The human somatosensory system: From perception to decision making" (2013) 103 *Progress in Neurobiology* 76–97, 81 [*Italics* added].

9 Bobby Chesney and Danielle Citron, "Deep Fakes: A Looming Challenge for Privacy, Democracy, and National Security" (2019) 107 *California Law Review* 1753–1820, 1819.

10 *Ibid.*

11 Mary L. Still and Jeremiah D. Still, "Subliminal Techniques: Considerations and Recommendations for Analyzing Feasibility" (2018) 34(5) *International Journal of Human–Computer Interaction* 457–466, 464–465.

12 Pamela K. Smith and Kathleen McCulloch, "Subliminal Perception" in V.S. Ramachandran (ed.), *Encyclopedia of Human Behavior*, vol. 1, 2nd ed. (London: Academic Press, 2012) 551–557, 551 [*Italics* added].

13 Kathryn Linn Geurts, *Culture and the Senses: Bodily Ways of Knowing in an African Community* (Berkeley, CA: University of California Press, 2002) 3.

14 Wataru Sato et al., "Cultural Moderation of Unconscious Hedonic Responses to Food" (2019) 11 *Nutrients* 1–9, 7.

15 Björnstjern Baade, "Fake News and International Law" (2019) 29 *The European Journal of International Law* 1357–1376 and Kate Klonick, "The Facebook Oversight Board: Creating an Independent Institution to Adjudicate Online Free Expression" (2020) 129(8) *Yale Law Journal* 2418–2499.

16 Nicolas Kayser-Bril, "European Council and Commission in agreement to narrow the scope of the AI Act", *Algorithm Watch* (23 November 2021); https://algorithmwatch.org/en/eu-narrow-scope-of-ai-act/.

17 Nathalie Smuha et al., "How the EU Can Achieve Legally Trustworthy AI: A Response to the European Commission's Proposal for an Artificial Intelligence Act." (2021), 21; https://papers.ssrn.com/sol3/papers.cfm?abstract_id=3899991, 21 and Mateja Durovic and Jonathon Watson, "Nothing to Be Happy about: Consumer Emotions and AI" (2021) 4(4) *J* 784–793, 792.

18 Future of Life Institute (FLI), *FLI Position Paper on the EU AI Act* (August 2021) 6; https://futureoflife.org/wp-content/uploads/2021/08/FLI-Position-Paper-on-the-EU-AI-Act.pdf?x72900.

19 *Ibid.*, 7.

20 *Ibid.*

21 Emma Cave, "Voluntary Vaccination: The Pandemic Effect" (2017) 37(2) *Legal Studies* 279–304, 282.

22 Bruce Schneier, *Data and Goliath: The Hidden Battles to Collect Your Data and Control Your World* (New York: W.W. Norton, 2015) 7.

23 David Throsby, "The Concentric Circles Model of the Cultural Industries" (2008) 17(3) *Cultural Trends* 147–164, 149.

24 Nicholas Garnham, "From Cultural to Creative Industries" (2005) 11(1) *International Journal of Cultural Policy* 15–29, 20.

25 Susan Galloway and Stewart Dunlop, "A Critique of Definitions of the Cultural and Creative industries in Public Policy" (2007) 13(1) *International Journal of Cultural Policy* 17–31, 19.

26 Rostam J. Neuwirth, "Global Market Integration and the Creative Economy: The Paradox of Industry Convergence and Regulatory Divergence" (2015) 18(1) *Journal of International Economic Law* 21–50, 29.

27 Fabio Ancarani and Michele Costabile, "Coopetition Dynamics in Convergent Industries: Designing Scope Connections to Combine Heterogeneous Resources" in Saïd Yami et al. (eds.), *Coopetition: Winning Strategies for the 21st Century* (Cheltenham: Edward Elgar, 2010) 216–237, 216.

28 Iria Giuffrida; Fredric Lederer, and Nicolas Vermeys, "A Legal Perspective on the Trials and Tribulations of AI: How Artificial Intelligence, the Internet of Things, Smart Contracts, and Other Technologies Will Affect the Law" (2018) 68(3) *Case Western Reserve Law Review* 747–782, 780.

29 Justin R. Schlosberg, *Media Ownership and Agenda Control: The Hidden Limits of the Information Age* (New York: Routledge, 2017) 8.

30 Mimo Draskovic, "Concentration of Media Ownership as a Global Phenomenon" (2011) 7(2) *Montenegrin Journal of Economics* 145–152, 145.

31 Jason Whittaker, *Tech Giants, Artificial Intelligence, and the Future of Journalism* (New York: Routledge, 2019) 4, Royston Greenwood and Roy Suddaby, "Institutional Entrepreneurship in Mature Fields: The Big Five Accounting Firms" (2006) 49(1) *The Academy of Management Journal* 27–48, 30.

32 Jennifer G. Hill, "The Conundrum of Common Ownership" (2020) 53(3) *Vanderbilt Journal of Transnational Law* 881–906, 881.

33 Ulrich Schwalbe, "Common Ownership and Competition – The Current State of the Debate" (2018) 9(9) *Journal of European Competition Law & Practice* 596–603, 603.

34 Harvey B. Feigenbaum, "The paradox of television privatization: When more is less" (2009) 27(3) *Policy and Society* 229–237, 229 and Kari Karppinen (ed.), *Rethinking Media Pluralism* (New York: Fordham University Press, 2012) 103–123.

35 Ronald E. Rice, "Artifacts and Paradoxes in New Media" (1999) 1(1) *New Media & Society* 24–32, 27–31.

36 Eli M. Noam, *Who Owns the World's Media? Media Concentration and Ownership around the World* (Oxford: Oxford University Press, 2016) 4.

37 Schlosberg, *supra* note 29, 153.

38 Gavin Ellis, *Trust Ownership and the Future of News: Media Moguls and White Knights* (New York: Palgrave Macmillan, 2014) 18.

39 United Nations Conference on Trade and Development (UNCTAD), *World Creative Economy Report 2010* (Geneva: UNCTAD, 2010) 10 and 28.

40 Christian Tietje, "Global Governance and Inter-Agency Co-operation in International Economic Law" (2002) 36(2) *Journal of World Trade* 501–515 and Margaret A. Young (ed.), *Regime Interaction in International Law: Facing Fragmentation* (Cambridge: Cambridge University Press, 2012).

41 Anupam Chander, "Future-Proofing Law" (2017) 51(1) *U.C. Davis Law Review* 1–25 and Sofia Ranchordás and Mattis van't Schip, "Future-Proofing Legislation for the Digital Age" in Sofia Ranchordás and Yaniv Roznai (eds.), *Time, Law, and Change: An Interdisciplinary Study* (Oxford: Hart Publishing, 2020) 347–365.

42 Neuwirth, "Global Market Integration and the Creative Economy", *supra* note 26, 29 and David Held, *Cosmopolitanism: Ideals and Realities* (Cambridge: Polity Press, 2010) 143.

43 Joseph A. Schumpeter, *Capitalism, Socialism and Democracy*, 2nd ed. (New York: Harper, 1947) 81–86.

44 Alexandre Senegacnik, "Expressio Unius (Est) Exclusio Alterius" in Hélène Ruiz Fabri (ed.), *Max Planck Encyclopedia of International Procedural Law* (Oxford: Oxford University Press, 2018) and H. Patrick Glenn, "Choice of Logic and Choice of Law" in H. Patrick Glenn and Lionel D. Smith (eds.), *Law and the New Logics* (Cambridge: Cambridge University Press, 2017) 162–167, 162.

45 Eric S. Rabkin, "Undecidability and Oxymoronism" in George E. Slusser and Tom A. Shippey (eds.), *Fiction 2000: Cyberpunk and the Future of Narrative* (Athens, GA: University of Georgia Press, 1992) 262–278, 265 and Timo Siivonen, "Cyborgs and Generic Oxymorons: The Body and Technology in William Gibson's Cyberspace Trilogy" (1996) 23(2) *Science Fiction Studies* 227–244, 227.

46 European Commission, *Proposal for a Regulation of the European Parliament and of the Council on contestable and fair markets in the digital sector (Digital Markets Act)*, COM(2020) 842 final (12 December 2020) [DMA].

47 European Commission, *Proposal for a Regulation of the European Parliament and of the Council on a Single Market For Digital Services (Digital Services Act) and amending Directive 2000/31/EC*, COM(2020) 825 final (15 December 2020) [DSA].

48 Council Directive 85/374/EEC (Product Liability Directive), OJ L 210/29 (7 August 1985) [PLD] and European Parliament, *Resolution of 20 October 2020 with recommendations to the Commission on a civil liability regime for artificial intelligence (2020/2014(INL))*, P9_TA(2020)0276 (20 October 2020).

49 Directive 2005/29/EC (Unfair Commercial Practices Directive), OJ L 149/22–39 (11 June 2005).

50 Directive 2000/31/EC (Electronic Commerce Directive), OJ L 178/1–16 (17 July 2000).

51 Directive (EU) 2018/1808 (Audiovisual Media Services Directive), OJ L 303/69–92 (28 November 2018) [*Italics* added] [AVMSD].

52 European Commission, *Europe's Media in the Digital Decade: An Action Plan to Support Recovery and Transformation*, COM(2020) 784 final (3 December 2020) 12.
53 Philipp Hacker, "Manipulation by Algorithms. Exploring the Triangle of Unfair Commercial Practice, Data Protection, and Privacy Law" (2021) *European Law Journal* 1–34, 28; https://doi.org/10.1111/eulj.12389 and Eliza Mik, "The erosion of autonomy in online consumer transactions" (2016) 8(1) Law, Innovation and Technology 1–38.
54 Steven Livingston and Mathias Risse, "The Future Impact of Artificial Intelligence on Humans and Human Rights" (2019) 33(2) *Ethics & International Affairs* 141–156, 155.
55 Nicolas Petit, "Antitrust and Artificial Intelligence: A Research Agenda" (2017) 8(6) *Journal of European Competition Law & Practice* 361–262 and Joseph E. Harrington, Jr., "Developing Competition Law for Collusion by Autonomous Artificial Agents" (2019) 14(3) *Journal of Competition Law & Economics* 331–363.
56 Stephanie Hoffer, "What if Tax Law's Future is Now? An Introduction to the Symposium on Artificial Intelligence & The Future of Tax Law" (2020) 16(1) *The Ohio State Technology Law Journal* 67–72.
57 Tom C.W. Lin, "Artificial Intelligence, Finance, and the Law" (2019) 88 (2) *Fordham Law Review* 531–552.
58 Hannah R. Sullivan and Scott J. Schweikart, "Are Current Tort Liability Doctrines Adequate for Addressing Injury Caused by AI?" (2019) 21(2) *AMA Journal of Ethics* E160–166.
59 Ryan Abbott and Alex Sarch, "Punishing Artificial Intelligence: Legal Fiction or Science Fiction" (2019) 53(1) *UC Davis Law Review* 323–384, 328 and Gabriel Hallevy, *Liability for Crimes Involving Artificial Intelligence Systems* (Cham: Springer International, 2015) 22.
60 Reto Hilty, Jyh-An Lee and Kung-Chung Liu (eds.), *Artificial Intelligence and Intellectual Property* (Oxford: Oxford University Press, 2021).
61 Shin-yi Peng, Ching-Fu Lin and Thomas Streinz (eds.), *Artificial Intelligence and International Economic Law: Disruption, Regulation, and Reconfiguration* (Cambridge: Cambridge University Press, 2021).
62 Ashley Deeks, "Introduction to the Symposium: How Will Artificial Intelligence Affect International Law?" (2020) 114 *American Journal of International Law Unbound* 138–140.
63 Peggy Valcke, Damian Clifford, and Vilte˙ Kristina Dessers, "Constitutional Challenges in the Emotional AI Era" in Hans-W. Micklitz et al. (eds.), *Constitutional Challenges in the Algorithmic Society* (Cambridge: Cambridge University Press, 2022) 57–77, 71 and Rostam J. Neuwirth, "The European Union as an Oxymoron: From Contest via Contradiction to Constitution?" in Julien Chaisse (ed.), *Sixty Years of European Integration and Global Power Shifts: Perceptions, Interactions and Lessons* (Oxford: Hart, 2019) 51–65, 57.
64 Gabriel A. Silva, "A New Frontier: The Convergence of Nanotechnology, Brain Machine Interfaces, and Artificial Intelligence" (2018) 12(843) *Frontiers in Neuroscience* 1–8; doi: 10.3389/fnins.2018.00843 and Yinong Chen, "IoT, cloud, big data and AI in interdisciplinary domains" (2020) 102 *Simulation Modelling Practice and Theory* 1–5; https://doi.org/10.1016/j.simpat.2020.102070.

65 Charles Handy, *The Age of Paradox* (Boston: Harvard Business School Press, 1995) x.

66 Helen Vendler, *The Music of What Happens: Poems, Poets, Critics* (Cambridge, MA: Harvard University Press, 1988) 242.

67 James N. Rosenau, "Governance in the 21st Century" (1995) 1(1) *Global Governance* 13–43, 13, Valentin Jeutner, *Irresolvable Norm Conflicts in International Law: The Concept of a Legal Dilemma* (Oxford: Oxford University Press, 2017), and Rostam J. Neuwirth, *Law in the Time of Oxymora: A Synaesthesia of Language, Logic and Law* (New York: Routledge, 2018).

68 Rostam J. Neuwirth, "The 'Letter' and 'Spirit' of Comparative Law in the Time of 'Artificial Intelligence' and other Oxymora" (2020) 26(1) *Canterbury Law Review* 1–31, 9–13.

69 Rostam J Neuwirth "Essentially Oxymoronic Concepts" (2013) 2(2) *Global Journal of Comparative Law* 147–166, 150.

70 Andreas Wagner, *Paradoxical Life: Meaning, Matter, and the Power of Human Choice* (New Haven: Yale University Press, 2009) 3.

71 Neuwirth, *Law in the Time of Oxymora, supra* note 67, 255.

72 Handy, *supra* note 65, xi.

73 Held, *supra* note 42, 143.

74 Esther Njiro, "Introduction: Sustainable Development an Oxymoron?" (2002) 52 *Agenda* 3–7.

75 Rostam J. Neuwirth, "GAIA 2048 – A 'Glocal Agency in Anthropocene': Cognitive and Institutional Change as 'Legal Science Fiction'", in Meredith Kolsky Lewis, Junji Nakagawa, Rostam J. Neuwirth, Colin B. Picker, and Peter-Tobias Stoll, (eds.), *A Post-WTO International Legal Order: Utopian, Dystopian and Other Scenarios* (Cham: Springer, 2020) 71–92.

76 Simon Chesterman, "Weapons of Mass Disruption: Artificial Intelligence and International Law", *NUS Law Working Paper 2021/009* (April 2021) 1; https://law.nus.edu.sg/wp-content/uploads/2021/05/009_2021_SimonC.pdf and Olivia J. Erdélyi and Judy Goldsmith, "Regulating Artificial Intelligence: Proposal for a Global Solution" (2018) *AIES '18: Proceedings of the 2018 AAAI/ACM Conference on AI, Ethics, and Society* 95–101, 100; https://doi.org/10.1145/3278721.3278731.

77 Erdélyi and Goldsmith, *ibid.*, 95.

78 Matthijs M. Maas, "International Law Does Not Compute: Artificial Intelligence and the Development, Displacement or Destruction of the Global Legal Order" (2019) 20(1) *Melbourne Journal of International Law* 29–57, 29 and 56.

79 Erdélyi and Goldsmith, *supra* note 76, 95 and 100.

80 Rostam J. Neuwirth, "The Fragmentation of the Global Market: The Case of Digital Versatile Discs (DVDs)" (2009) 27 *Cardozo Arts & Entertainment Law Journal* 409–458, Marketa Trimble, "The Future of Cybertravel: Legal Implications of the Evasion of Geolocation" (2012) 22(3) *Fordham Intellectual Property Media and Entertainment Law Journal* 567–657, 569–570, Peter K. Yu, "A Hater's Guide to Geoblocking" (2019) 25(2) *Boston University Journal of Science and Technology Law* 503–529 and European Commission, *Geo-Blocking Practices in e-Commerce*, SWD(2016) 70 final (18 March 2016).

81 Baade, *supra* note 15, Rostam J. Neuwirth, "The Regulation of 'Fake News' in the Time of Oxymora: Facts and Fictions about the Covid-19 Pandemic as Coincidences or Predictive Programming?" (2021) *International Journal for the Semiotics of Law* 1–27; https://doi.org/10.1007/s11196-021-09840-y, and the *Convention on the International Right of Correction*, New York, 31 March 1953, 435 UNTS 191.

82 George P. Fletcher, "Paradoxes in Legal Thought" (1985) 85(6) *Columbia Law Review* 1263–1292, 1292.

83 John Dewey, "Logical Method and Law" (1924) 10(1) *Cornell Law Quarterly* 17–27, 26.

84 Pier Luigi Gentili, "Establishing a New Link between Fuzzy Logic, Neuroscience, and Quantum Mechanics through Bayesian Probability: Perspectives in Artificial Intelligence and Unconventional Computing" (2021) 26(5987) *Molecules* 1–18, 1; https://doi.org/10.3390/molecules26195987 and Lotfi A. Zadeh, "Fuzzy Logic = Computing with Words" (1996) 4(2) *IEEE Transactions on Fuzzy Systems* 103–111.

85 Narinder Kapur et al., "The Paradoxical Nature of Nature" in Narinder Kapur (ed.), *The Paradoxical Brain* (Cambridge: Cambridge University Press, 2011) 1–13, 1.

86 Steve J. Stern and Scott Straus, "Embracing Paradox: Human Rights in the Global Age" in Steve J. Stern and Scott Straus (eds.), *The Human Rights Paradox: Universality and its Discontents* (Madison, WI: The University of Wisconsin Press, 2014) 3–28, 3.

87 *International Covenant on Civil and Political Rights*, 16 December 1966, 999 U.N.T.S. 171 [ICCPR] and *International Covenant on Economic, Social and Cultural Rights*, 16 December 1966, 993 U.N.T.S. 3 [ICESCR].

88 Gerard Guinn, "The European Union and the Council of Europe on the Issue of Human Rights: Twins Separated at Birth" (2001) 46(4) *McGill Law Journal* 849–874.

89 Art. 18 ICCPR, *supra* note 87; Art. 9 *European Convention for the Protection of Human Rights and Fundamental Freedoms*, 4 November 1950, ETS 5; and Art. 10 *Charter of Fundamental Rights of the European Union*, OJ C 326/391–407 (26 October 2012) [CFR].

90 *Universal Declaration of Human Rights*, GA Res 217 A (III) (adopted 10 December 1948) [UDHR].

91 Jan Christoph Bublitz, "Freedom of Thought in the Age of Neuroscience: A Plea and a Proposal for the Renaissance of a Forgotten Fundamental Right" (2014) 100(1) *Archiv für Rechts- und Sozialphilosophie* 1–25, 12.

92 Marcia J. Bates, "Fundamental Forms of Information" (2006) 57(8) *The Journal of the Association for Information Science and Technology* 1033–1045, 1033.

93 Ervin Laszlo, *Science and the Akashic Field: An Integral Theory of Everything*, 2nd ed. (Rochester, VT: Inner Traditions, 2007) 13.

94 Raghunath Tiruvaipati, *Information Theory of the Cosmos: How the New Science of Information Changes Our Understanding and Perception of the Universe* (New Delhi: Educreation, 2018) viii.

95 Bublitz, *supra* note 91, 12.

96 *Ibid.*

97 Art. 19 UDHR, *supra* note 90 [*Italics* added]. Cf. Art. 11 CFR, *supra* note 89.
98 William J. Stewart, "Stimulating Intuitive Thinking through Problem Solving" (1988) 62(4) *The Clearing House* 175–176.
99 Raul Espejo, "What Is Systemic Thinking?" (1994) 10(2–3) *System Dynamics Review* 199–212.
100 John Adair, *The Art of Creative Thinking: How to Be Innovative and Develop Great Ideas* (London: Kogan Page, 2007).
101 Jerry L. Fletcher, *Paradoxical Thinking: How to Profit from Your Contradictions* (San Francisco: Berrett-Koehler Publishers, 1997).
102 Neuwirth, *Law in the Time of Oxymora, supra* note 67, 121, 125, 173 and 179.
103 Jeutner, *supra* note 67, 93 *et seq.*
104 Jeffery Atik and Valentin Jeutner, "Quantum Computing and Computational Law" (2021) 13 *Law, Innovation and Technology* 302–324, 314.
105 Benjamin N. Cardozo, *The Paradoxes of Legal Science* (New York: Columbia University Press, 1928) 4–5.
106 Bart Kosko, *Fuzzy Thinking: The New Science of Fuzzy Logic* (New York: Hyperion, 1993) 21.
107 Iris Eisenberger, *Innovation im Recht* (Wien: Verlag Österreich, 2016) 156–157.
108 Vincent M. Guibout and Daniel J. Scheeres, "Solving Two-Point Boundary Value Problems Using Generating Functions: Theory and Applications to Astrodynamics" in Pini Gurfil (ed.), *Modern Astrodynamics* (Amsterdam: Elsevier, 2007) 53.
109 Gloria González Fuster, *The Emergence of Personal Data Protection as a Fundamental Right of the EU* (Cham: Springer International, 2014) 14.
110 Art. 8 CFR, *supra* note 89.
111 Art. 25 UDHR, *supra* note 90; Art. 12 ICESCR, *supra* note 87.
112 UNESCO International Bioethics Committee (IBC), *Preliminary Draft Report of the IBC on Ethical Issues of Neurotechnology*, SHS/BIO/IBC-Ext/2021/3 (15 December 2020) 14–15.
113 John-Dylan Haynes, "Brain Reading" in Sarah D. Richmond, Geraint Rees, and Sarah J. L. Edwards (eds.), *I Know What You're Thinking: Brain Imaging and Mental Privacy* (Oxford: Oxford University Press, 2012) 34–40, 38.
114 UNESCO International Bioethics Committee (IBC), *supra* note 112, 14–15 [*Italics* added].
115 Lewis Carroll, *Through the Looking Glass, and What Alice Found There* (London: MacMillan, 1872) 127.
116 Jen Doll, "Now We're Just Making Stuff Up: A Guide to the Rise of the Portmanteau", *The Atlantic* (15 September 2012); https://www.theatlantic.com/culture/archive/2012/09/now-were-just-making-it-guide-rise-portmanteauing/323626/.
117 Börje Johansson· Charlie Karlsson and Lars Westin (eds.), *Patterns of a Network Economy* (Berlin: Springer, 1994).
118 Erik Brynjolfsson and Brian Kahin (eds.), *Understanding the Digital Economy: Data, Tools, and Research* (Cambridge, MA: MIT Press, 2000).
119 Arun Sundararajan, *The Sharing Economy: The End of Employment and the Rise of Crowd-Based Capitalism* (Cambridge, MA: MIT Press, 2016).

120 José María Cavanillas, Edward Curry, and Wolfgang Wahlster (eds.), *New Horizons for a Data-Driven Economy: A Roadmap for Usage and Exploitation of Big Data in Europe* (Cham: Springer 2016).

121 George Gilder, *Life After Google: The Fall of Big Data and the Rise of the Blockchain Economy* (Washington: Regnery Gateway, 2018).

122 Joseph B. Pine and James J. Gilmore, *The Experience Economy: Work is Theatre & Every Business a Stage* (Boston: Harvard Business School Press, 1999).

123 John Howkins, *The Creative Economy: How People Make Money from Ideas* (London: Penguin, 2002).

124 Jelena Danilović Jeremić and Jelena Josijević, "To blend so as to brand: a study of trademarks and brand names" (2019) 14 *Lexis* 1–19; https://doi.org/10.4000/lexis.3732.

125 Mark Tunner and Fauconnier, "Conceptual Integration and Formal Expression" (1995) 10(3) *Metaphor and Symbolic Activity* 183–204, 183.

126 Dirk Helbing, *Next Civilization: Digital Democracy and Socio-Ecological Finance—How to Avoid Dystopia and Upgrade Society by Digital Means*, 2nd ed. (Cham: Springer, 2021) 63.

127 *Ibid.*, 65.

128 Pierre Lepaulle, "The Function of Comparative Law with a Critique of Sociological Jurisprudence" (1922) 35(7) *Harvard Law Review* 838–858, 838.

129 Lon L. Fuller, "On Teaching Law" (1950) 3(1) *Stanford Law Review* 35–47, 37.

130 Ludwig Wittgenstein, *Tractatus Logico-Philosophicus* (London: Routledge, 1960) 43 (3.02).

131 Andrew T.F. Lang, "Reflecting on 'Linkage': Cognitive and Institutional Change in the International Trading System" (2007) 70(4) *Modern Law Review* 523–549, 529.

132 Sarah Marusek, "Exploring Layers of Law and the Sensory at the Volcano" in Sarah Marusek (ed.), *Synesthetic Legalities: Sensory Dimensions of Law and Jurisprudence* (Abingdon, Oxon: Routledge, 2017) 1–8, 1.

133 Neuwirth, *Law in the Time of Oxymora, supra* note 67, xiv.

134 Lawrence E. Marks, *The Unity of the Senses: Interrelations among the Modalities* (New York: Academic Press, 1978) 182.

135 Sean Day, "Synaesthesia and Synaesthetic Metaphors" (1996) 2(32) *Psyche* 1–19, 1.

136 Yeshayahu Shen and Michael Cohen, "How Come Silence is Sweet but Sweetness is not Silent: A Cognitive Account of Directionality in Poetic Synaesthesia" (1998) 7(1) *Language and Literature* 123–140, 139.

137 Brian Bix, *Law, Language, and Legal Determinacy* (Oxford: Clarendon Press, 2003) 1.

138 George Lakoff and Mark Johnson, *Metaphors We Live By* (Chicago: The University of Chicago Press, 1980) 3.

139 Rostam J. Neuwirth, "Legal Semiotics and Synaesthesia" in Anne Wagner and Sarah Marusek (eds.), *Research Handbook on Legal Semiotics* (Cheltenham: Edward Elgar, forthcoming in 2023).

140 David Crystal, *A Dictionary of Linguistics and Phonetics*, 6th ed. (Malden, MA: Blackwell, 2008) 431.

141 Susan Tiefenbrun, *Decoding International Law: Semiotics and the Humanities* (Oxford: Oxford University Press, 2010) 20.

142 Manuela Epure, Eric Eisenstat, and Christina Dinu, "Semiotics and Persuasion in Marketing Communication" (2014) 13 *Linguistic and Philosophical Investigations* 592–605.
143 Diane Ackerman, *A Natural History of the Senses* (New York: Vintage Books, 1990) xvii.
144 Rostam J. Neuwirth, "International Adjudication and Semiotics" in Hélène Ruiz Fabri (ed.), *Max Planck Encyclopedia of International Procedural Law (MPEiPro)* (Oxford: Oxford University Press, 2021) 1–30, Neal Feigenson and Christina Spiesel, *Law on Display: The Digital Transformation of Legal Persuasion and Judgment* (New York: New University Press, 2009) and Elizabeth G Porter, "Taking Images Seriously" (2014) 114(7) *Columbia Law Review* 1687–1782.
145 Lionel Bently, "Introduction" in Lionel Bently and Leo Flynn (eds.), *Law and the Senses: Sensational Jurisprudence* (London: Pluto Press, 1996), 3.
146 Neuwirth, "International Adjudication and Semiotics", *supra* note 144 and Luca Pasquet, "De-Fragmentation Techniques" in Hélène Ruiz Fabri (ed.), *Max Planck Encyclopedia of International Procedural Law (MPEiPro)* (Oxford: Oxford University Press, 2021).
147 Anne Wagner, "Mapping legal semiotics" (2010) 23 *International Journal for the Semiotics of Law* 77–82, 78.
148 Jeff Chester, "Cookie Wars: How New Data Profiling and Targeting Techniques Threaten Citizens and Consumers in the 'Big Data' Era" in Serge Gutwirth et al. (eds.), *European Data Protection: In Good Health?* (Dordrecht: Springer, 2012) 53–77, 53–55.
149 Basarab Nicolescu, "The Need for Transdisciplinarity in Higher Education in a Globalized World" (2012) 3 *Transdisciplinary Journal of Engineering & Science* 11–18, 11.
150 Yuval Noah Harari, *Homo Deus: A Brief History of Tomorrow* (New York: Harper, 2017), 51.
151 David De Cremer and Garry Kasparov, "AI Should Augment Human Intelligence, Not Replace It", *Harvard Business Review* (18 March 2021); https://hbr.org/2021/03/ai-should-augment-human-intelligence-not-replace-it; Garry Kasparov, *Deep Thinking: Where Machine Intelligence Ends and Human Creativity Begins* (New York: PublicAffairs, 2017) 259.
152 David J. Epstein, *Range: Why Generalists Triumph in a Specialized World* (New York: Riverhead Books, 2019) 29.
153 Hans Moravec, *Mind Children: The Future of Robot and Human Intelligence* (Boston: Harvard University Press, 1988) 15.
154 A quoted cited from a Tweet by the Centre for AI and Digital Ethics (@CAIDE_UoM) (2 December 2021) apparently attributed to Tim Miller (tmiller@unimelb); https://twitter.com/CAIDE_UoM/status/1466242971196526601.
155 Kenneth L. Mossman, *The Complexity Paradox: The More Answers We Find, the More Questions We Have* (Oxford: Oxford University Press, 2014).
156 Henry Prakken, "Logics of Argumentation and the Law" in H. Patrick Glenn and Lionel D. Smith (eds.), *Law and the New Logics* (Cambridge: Cambridge University Press, 2017) 3–31, 3.
157 Isaac Asimov, "My Own View" in Robert Holdstock (ed.), *The Encyclopedia of Science Fiction* (London: Octopus, 1978) 5, 5.

158 Jon Truby et al., "A Sandbox Approach to Regulating High-Risk Artificial Intelligence Applications" (2021) *European Journal of Risk Regulation* 1–29; doi:10.1017/err.2021.52.

159 Carlo Rovelli, *The Order of Time* (New York: Riverhead Books, 2018) 111.

160 Maynard Rolston, *Time Management Is an Oxymoron: Learn How to Get More Done in Less Time* (Leawood, KS: Leathers Publishing, 2001) 86.

161 Robert John Russell, *Time in Eternity: Pannenberg, Physics, and Eschatology in Creative Mutual Interaction* (Notre Dame, IN: University of Notre Dame Press, 2012) 260.

162 Heather Mann et al., "Time–space synaesthesia – A cognitive advantage?" (2009) 18 *Consciousness and Cognition* 619–627, 619 and 625.

163 Neuwirth, *Law in the Time of Oxymora, supra* note 67, 259 and Charles H. Hinton, *The Fourth Dimension* (London: Swan Sonnenschein & Co., 1901).

164 William Shakespeare, "Hamlet" in John Dover Wilson (ed.), *The Works of William Shakespeare*, vol. 7 (Cambridge: Cambridge University Press, 2009) 3, 62 [*Italics* added].

165 Thomas H. Davenport, *The AI Advantage: How to Put the Artificial Intelligence Revolution to Work* (Cambridge, MA: The MIT Press, 2018) 7.

Conclusion

> *The conscious and intelligent manipulation of the organized habits and opinions of the masses is an important element in democratic society. Those who manipulate this unseen mechanism of society constitute an invisible government which is the true ruling power of our country.*[1]

Technology has always influenced and shaped our lives. In this regard, there is nothing new under the sun. In fact, it is hard to imagine anything being created from nothing. However, time and again, new technologies initially appear novel in terms of their inherent opportunities but later reveal their serious risks. Today, the fundamental novelty of the new technologies broadly circumscribed by AI lie largely in the creation of intelligent machines. We are only slowly realising the dangers of the hidden manipulation of the deepest thoughts and cognitive processes in the human brain. In this regard, one aspect of technology that is too often forgotten is that any tool, even the simplest prehistoric tool, has always had and will always have an impact on the mind of its user. This phenomenon can be explained by the conceptualisation of different technologies functioning as extensions of the human body and the concept of *homo faber* or the human being as the artisan of her/his own destiny. However, in order to shape one's own destiny, one's mind must – paradoxically – be controlled but at same time kept free from unwanted manipulative practices by third parties. Obviously, it is every individual's responsibility to control their own mind, but it is society's task to ensure that individuals' minds are not being manipulated in secretive and harmful ways.

Against this background, the European Commission's proposal for an AIA must be welcomed as an important comprehensive regulatory initiative that aims to tackle the challenges of existing and future technologies paraphrased as "artificial intelligence". The importance stems from the fact that even the most specific technical devices and

DOI: 10.4324/9781003319436-5

inventions existing today already pose serious ethical concerns in their application. This trend will only be exacerbated in the future with the further convergence between different systems, industries, technologies, and applications. There is thus good reason to opt for the creation of a binding legal framework for systems as powerful as those of AI, because of their ubiquitous and still-expanding role in the lives of present and future generations.

For this reason, the parallel efforts between states and by various regional and international organisations, such as the Council of Europe, the OECD, and UNESCO, to subject the development of artificial intelligence systems to a binding legal framework are crucial. In line with the paradox of our times, it is clear that a global standard-setting instrument must also be realised in the near future so as to allow everyone on the planet to have access to the beneficial aspects of the novel technologies covered by this instrument but to be free, or protected, from its serious risks and dangers.

The AIA also reflects a good amount of critical foresight, because among the opportunities associated with the technologies called "AI" come the serious dangers of their hidden interference with the brain and mind enabled by various neurotechnologies like BCI or fMRI. Therefore, from the perspective of the mind, perhaps the greatest value of the AIA lies in the planned specific prohibition of any "AI system that deploys subliminal techniques beyond a person's consciousness". Judging from past experience with a similar prohibition on subliminal advertising and with the support of recent scientific experiments that have generally confirmed the effect of subliminal stimuli or so-called "hidden persuaders" on not only the mind but also the actions of humans, this planned prohibition, regardless of possible amendments made to the draft and its final wording, is definitely a step in the right direction and should be introduced in every jurisdiction. Even just the popularity of subliminal content on various video platforms offered for a variety of purposes, including self-help (e.g. to boost confidence, happiness or motivation), meditation, and learning (e.g. as exam preparation) seems to require some regulatory attention to this subject. Already, there exist technologies or devices termed "brain spyware" that apply subliminal techniques to get access to personal data and private thoughts. Therefore, it is only possible for the proposed regulation to raise awareness about these dangers prior to the development of future technologies of that sort, which is essential for guarding our minds against negative, harmful, and manipulative practices.

To give a brief summary here, it is first important to consider the wider context of the AIA and its relationship to other existing (as well as planned future) regulatory acts such as, notably, the GDPR, the PLD, the DMA, and the DSA. At the same time, it is important to rethink, in a creative way, the interaction between different legal fields such as competition law, intellectual property law, and international trade law or, to put it simply, the coherence and consistency of the legal system as a whole. In this context, regulators encounter the paradox that less, but better coordinated, regulation can achieve much more and do it better too.

Second, it is extremely important to concretise the plans for the enforcement of the entire AIA, as well as, in particular, specifying the competent authority or authorities and the (technological) means for monitoring AI systems for their potential deployment of subliminal techniques. Looking at the case of subliminal advertising, it is clear that there are imbalances between strong regulation and weak enforcement and between the large number of regulatory authorities and the small number of cases or infringements recorded. If no such actions are taken, the proposed article will lose its teeth and have no effect on the future development of AI systems falling into this category. In other words, there is also a need to correct the current imbalance in the use of surveillance technologies to, on the one hand, detect subliminal techniques and, on the other, to survey people. This is critically captured by the notion of surveillance capitalism, which "unilaterally claims human experience as free raw material for translation into behavioral data".[2]

Third, the analysis and discussion of the role of subliminal and supraliminal perception in human lives also underlines the importance of the role of the mind in life, science, technology, and law. In this respect, recent changes in language, noticeable in the form of the frequent use of oxymora and paradoxes, match recent changes in technology and indicate an imminent paradigm shift. Moreover, as reflected in the term "legal synaesthesia", they indicate the need for fundamental changes in the way law is conceptualised and applied beyond the traditional limitations imposed by dualistic reasoning and binary logic. It has been found that only when cognitive change materialises can the architecture of institutions be adapted to present and future needs.

All these elements taken together explain why the AIA and its prohibition of subliminal techniques provides a useful starting point for an important public global debate that supports calls for further and more interdisciplinary research, as well as flanking measures aimed at maintaining an open mind protected from its enemies. Such an open mind, free from hidden and harmful interventions, is essential for the protection of the privacy of citizens' thoughts. Otherwise the year 1984 marks not only the year that private life came to an end but also the year that *private thought came to an end*.[3] This is why the right to freedom of thought must receive greater attention as the ultimate and most fundamental precondition for the autonomy of human decision-making, otherwise known as "free will". Free will is the expression of the autonomy of decision-making and must also be safeguarded to preserve our human dignity digitally.

Notes

1 Edward Bernays, *Propaganda* (New York: Liveright, 1928) 9.
2 Shoshana Zuboff, *The Age of Surveillance Capitalism: The Fight for a Human Future at the New Frontier of Power* (New York: PublicAffairs, 2019) 8.
3 George Orwell, *1984* (New York: Signet, 1950) 156.

Index